I0104961

Quarterly Essay

iii Introduction *Peter Craven*

viii Map of West Papua

ix Glossary

1 PARADISE BETRAYED
West Papua's Struggle for Independence
John Martinkus

84 BEYOND BELIEF Correspondence
Kenneth Davidson, David Day, Barry Jones, Susan Ryan,
Hugh Stretton, John Button

132 Contributors

Quarterly Essay is published four times a year by Black Inc., an imprint of Schwartz Books Pty Ltd.
Publisher: Morry Schwartz.

ISBN 9781863951630 ISSN 1832-0953

Subscriptions – 1 year print & digital (4 issues): $79.95 within Australia incl. GST. Outside Australia $119.95. 2 years print & digital (8 issues): $149.95 within Australia incl. GST. 1 year digital only: $49.95.

Payment may be made by Mastercard or Visa, or by cheque made out to Schwartz Books. Payment includes postage and handling.

To subscribe, fill out and post the subscription card or form inside this issue, or subscribe online:

quarterlyessay.com
subscribe@blackincbooks.com
Phone: 61 3 9486 0288

Correspondence should be addressed to:

The Editor, Quarterly Essay
Level 1, 221 Drummond Street
Carlton VIC 3053 Australia
Phone: 61 3 9486 0288 / Fax: 61 3 9011 6106
Email: quarterlyessay@blackincbooks.com

Editor: Peter Craven
Management: Silvia Kwon
Managing Editor: Chris Feik
Production Coordinator: Sophy Williams
Publicity: Meredith Kelly
Design: Guy Mirabella
Map of West Papua: John Waddingham
West Papua photos: John Martinkus

Quarterly Essay aims to present significant contributions to political, intellectual and cultural debate. It is a magazine in extended pamphlet form and by publishing in each issue a single writer at a length of at least 20,000 words we hope to mediate between the limitations of the newspaper column, where there is the danger that evidence and argument can be swallowed up by the form, and the kind of full-length study of a subject where the only readership is a necessarily specialised one. *Quarterly Essay* aims for the attention of the committed general reader. Although it is a periodical which wants subscribers, each number of the journal is the length of a short book because we want our writers to have the opportunity to speak to the broadest possible audience without condescension or populist short-cuts. *Quarterly Essay* wants to get away from the tyranny that space limits impose in contemporary journalism and we give our essayists the space to express the evidence for their views and those who disagree with them the chance to reply at whatever length is necessary. *Quarterly Essay* will not be confined to politics but is centrally concerned with it. We are not interested in occupying any particular point on the political map and we hope to bring our readership the widest range of political and cultural opinion which is compatible with truth-telling, style and command of the essay form.

INTRODUCTION

In 1999 when John Howard went to the rescue of the people of East Timor, he finally brought Australian government policy in line with the feelings of the Australian people who had always taken the dimmest view of what the Indonesians had done to that poor brave put-upon country. And in the wake of the vote for independence when the militias backed by the brutality of the Indonesian military caused their wave of bloodshed and mayhem, middle-class mothers took to the streets of Sydney and Melbourne as they had not done since the height of the Vietnam War. They wanted an end to the killing, they wanted what Howard ultimately gave them, boots on the ground, for the sake of peace and the protection of life. They also wanted an end to twenty-five years of bipartisan Australian government hypocrisy.

In the new *Quarterly Essay* John Martinkus, who has written with such authority on East Timor, provides a path-breaking piece of extended reportage in which he shows that West Papua is another East Timor waiting to happen, that in fact it is happening with the collusion of Australia and American indifference and that the repression of the independence movement in West Papua is being effected by the very same Indonesian architects of bloodshed and oppression who produced the rape of East Timor.

John Martinkus is one of those foreign correspondents who risks his all to get the story, and *Paradise Betrayed* unfolds step by step as a riveting and disquieting narrative account of what it is like to visit what was almost a lost world before it encountered the Javanese will to power and denial of freedom.

He is absolutely level and absolutely convincing in the way he evokes the almost Australian familiarity of Vanimo with its takeaway food and its Rugby League on TV and then proceeds to hit the reader with the stomach-turning details of the torture and mutilation and carnage that has been inflicted on those who support the Papuan independence movement (the OPM as it is called) and raise the Morning Star flag that betokens their freedom. This is our back door, what should be our sphere of influence, on which the severed body parts fall.

It is a sobering and shocking story as Martinkus tells it and what stares through it is the dignity and simplicity of these warriors who have willed themselves to fight a cruel colonial regime in the face of little organisation or hope.

John Martinkus is lucid in his exposition of how the West Papuans were sold out to the Indonesians by US and Australian governments full of Cold War anxiety and he is scathing about the shibboleth of the "Free Choice" referendum and the current sop of autonomy which the Indonesians use to cover a regimen of exploitative cruelty.

We see the faces of the old men who worked for the UN and who saw their hopes drain into the sea just as we hear the story of Theys Eluay, the one figure around whom the independence movement clustered, who was murdered by the most feared unit of the Indonesian military machine, *Kopassus*. His far more temporising successor, Beanal, has seemed willing to do some kind of a deal with the Indonesians but even so there is little hope of mercy from a Jakartan government which has been bought off by the owners of the Freeport mine, one of the richest of its kind in the world and one whose commercial interests are safeguarded by Indonesian thuggery in a way that would sound like a Marxist caricature from the sixties if the sober Martinkus were not our informant.

This is a group portrait of people the world has chosen to forget, who have been offered next to nothing by an intimately familiar oppressor.

The autonomy the Indonesians proffer to the people of what used to be called Irian Jaya has some small appeal to the elites of West Papua but it offers nothing to the people some of whose first contact with the outside world took the form of the hostile faces of the Indonesian soldiers. They hunger for the freedom the Indonesians deny them by killing their leaders.

Martinkus has a remarkable scene in which he depicts the US Ambassador, a man of apparently liberal feeling, indicating to people who are as oppressed by fear as they are by death (the two as linked as the gun and its discharge) that no, it's not antagonism to the West Papuan people that governs policy, it's the lure of what comes out of the mine. It is Freeport that sits like an emblem of globalised greed on this ancient landscape and it will be hard for any reader of John Martinkus' *Quarterly Essay* not to see it as a sink of iniquity and an outright provocation. The fact that the West Papuans are capable of responding with explosive-tipped arrows does not stop the situation from being ghastly any more than the local colour that abounds in John Martinkus' account, with its penis-gourd-adorned Dani people who whoop like sirens as they wave their spears, stops this story from being one of pity and terror.

The terror is manifest on the cowed faces of the burly students who witnessed the Indonesian reprisals in the incident at the Abepura police station, with the blood dripping down the walls, and it is there, almost uncannily, when we read of how the Indonesians have sponsored Laskar Jihad, a group of sword-wielding, cloak-wearing Islamic extremists who have been sent into the country to teach the Papuans what's what.

John Martinkus' narrative is as engrossing as it is appalling. It is full of menace and madness and the smell of death. It is a story that involves malignancy just as it can seem, on the Papuan side, to exhibit a quixotic nobility in the face of futility. Still they continue to raise their Morning Star flag, still they are cut down like flowers.

John Martinkus is meticulous in his detailing of how the Dutch had foreshadowed the absorption of West Papua into the rest of Papua New

Guinea to which it is linked by race and culture. He delineates how our own government went along with the Kennedy administration in offering these people to the Indonesian Cerberus and he is sobering – desolatingly so – in suggesting that nobody, not Kofi Annan, not the Australians, not even Jose Ramos Horta, will offer these people any hope.

And through the whole, sometimes nearly comic, saga there is the whisper of death and the portent of death, of much more killing to come.

This is not a *Quarterly Essay* that takes a high line on foreign policy though its implications are clear enough. No one will lift a finger for the West Papuans against the very same Indonesian military leaders who have escaped (by and large) justice over East Timor. The West Papuans will be and are being mown down like grass by a regime which the people of Australia (with just cause) do not love.

If this situation continues it will become intolerable to people here and rightly so. John Martinkus has written a searing indictment which is primarily a piece of completely convincing reportage – reportage of the skin-of-the-teeth variety that can cost not less than everything. He tells it with a lack of rhetoric and with a concentration on the facts which he gathers as painstakingly as any hunter/gatherer who searched the earth for the means of survival.

This is foreign correspondence work with danger breathing down the author's neck at every turn. It will alter the picture of West Papua and it will carry conviction.

It is the very absence of eloquence, the plain reporter's style with its flashes of quiet humour in the face of a subject at once exotic and humanly ghastly, that makes *Paradise Betrayed* so powerful.

Conrad said that the purpose of fiction was to make the reader see. John Martinkus realises the same aim in this devastating essay which should galvanise opinion about the wrongs we are willing to see suffered on innocent and oppressed people.

A couple of years ago David Malouf said with some wisdom that the people in the region Australians care most deeply about are the people of

East Timor and the people of Papua New Guinea and that this is sacred to us because of the bond of war.

That Morning Star flag was being flown when the Japanese were hoping to fly their own over this part of the world. It may be a limited perspective but we could do worse in the face of evidence of outrage than ponder the image of how deeply the Papuan people go in the Australian memory.

Peter Craven

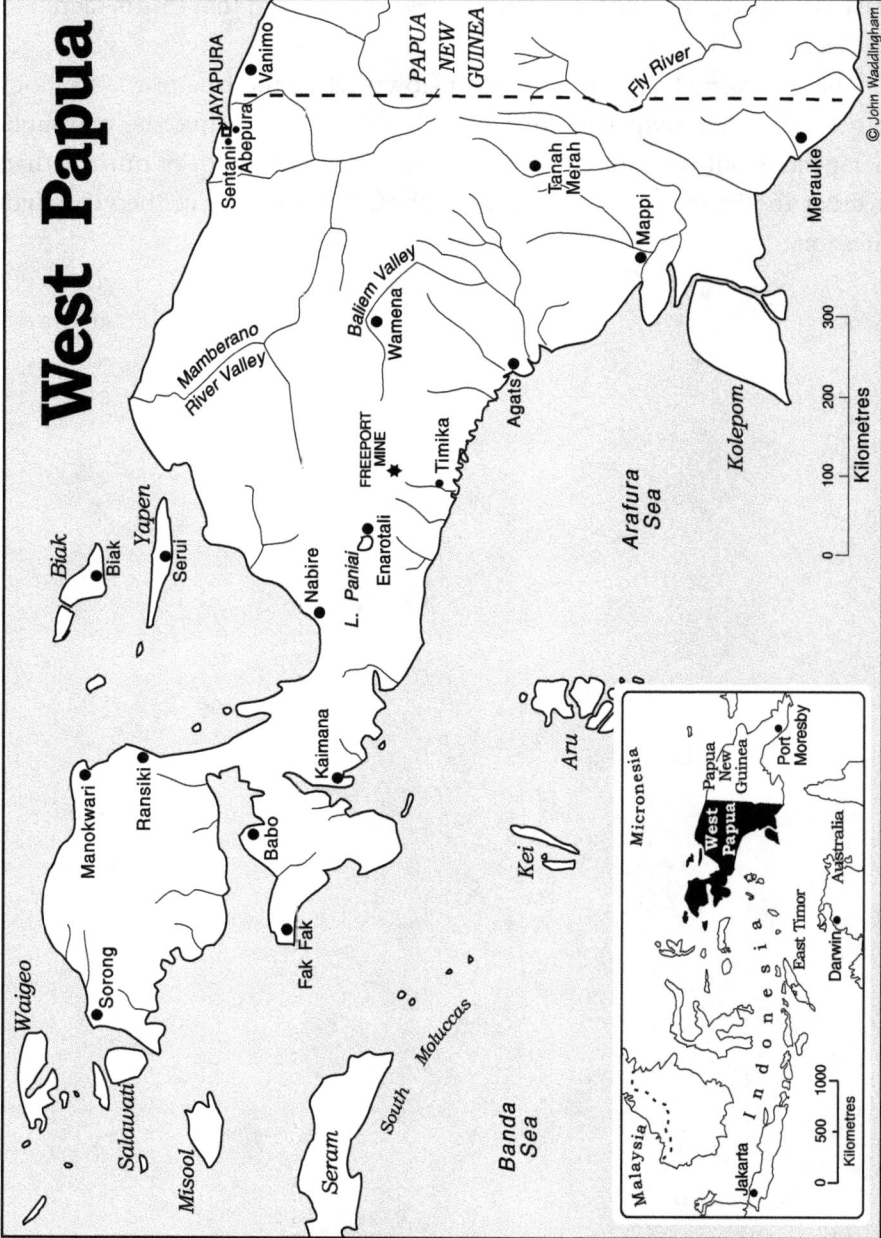

GLOSSARY

ACT OF FREE CHOICE	Referendum in 1969 which led to West Papua's integration into the Republic of Indonesia
ADAT COUNCIL	Indonesian-sponsored council of traditional leaders
BRIMOB	*Brigada Mobil*: Police Mobile Brigade, Indonesian riot police
DEMMAK	Political organisation of highlanders of West Papua
ELS-HAM	Institute for Human Rights Study and Advocacy, West Papua
GERAKAN MERAH PUTIH	Pro-integrationist militia
ICRC	International Committee of the Red Cross
KOPASSUS	Indonesian Special Forces
KOSTRAD	Strategic Reserve Command of the Indonesian Army
KPP-HAM	Commission of Inquiry into Human Rights Violations in East Timor
LASKAR JIHAD	Muslim militant group
OPM	*Organisasi Papua Merdeka*: Free Papua Movement, umbrella group for West Papuan resistance movement.
OPM-TPM	*Tentara Pembebasan Nasional*: Armed wing of West Papuan resistance movement.
PEPERA	Papuan name for the Act of Free Choice
PNGDF	Papua New Guinea Defence Force
PRESIDIUM COUNCIL	Elected council representing the Papuan people
SATGAS PAPUA	Papua Taskforce, a pro-independence militia
SATGAS MERAH PUTIH	Pro-integrationist militia
TNI	*Tentara Nasional Indonesia*: Indonesian Regular Army
UNTEA	United Nations transitional authority set up to oversee 1962 transfer
YLBH	Indonesian Legal Aid Foundation, Jakarta-based legal aid foundation

The author with OPM fighters at a secret border training camp on the PNG–West Papua border.

PARADISE BETRAYED

West Papua's Struggle for Independence

John Martinkus

The arrival of Australian troops in East Timor in September 1999 sent such a clear signal to the Indonesian settlers in West Papua that 60,000 of them left for other parts of Indonesia. It seemed at the time that independence for West Papua, the other province of Indonesia that had been forcibly integrated into the unitary republic back in 1962, was just a matter of time.

The parallels between West Papua and East Timor were obvious. Both had been taken over by Indonesia on very shaky legal grounds. Both had identified strongly with their former European colonial masters, the Papuans with the Dutch and the East Timorese with the Portuguese. And in each case their integration into neighbouring Indonesia was approved by the United States and Australia as part of the Cold War strategy to keep Indonesia out of the communist camp.

Both territories had suffered the full force of the Indonesian military's attempt to crush any resistance. In West Papua this left at least 100,000 people dead and inspired a legacy of hatred for the Indonesians that fuelled the independence movement.

In 1969, the Act of Free Choice, a sham plebiscite that allowed only 1,026 representatives chosen by the Indonesians from an indigenous population of 814,000 to vote on whether to remain a part of Indonesia, had apparently consigned West Papua to permanent occupation. But in 1999, as the Indonesian occupation of East Timor drew to a bloody close (and the Australian and American governments were finally compelled to condemn the actions of the Indonesian military), it seemed that the other great historical wrong to Australia's north might finally be redressed.

A wave of support for independence went through West Papua. The Morning Star flag, the emblem of Papuan independence, was flown for the first time without bloodshed, and massive rallies for self-government took place in the capital Jayapura, culminating in the 2nd Congress of West Papua in June 2000. For the time being the Indonesian military did not respond. Theys Eluay, leader of the Papuan Presidium Council, could credibly claim to speak for all Papuans when he demanded a UN-sponsored referendum for the people of West Papua to decide whether to remain a part of Indonesia.

But the Indonesian military was not idle for long. Militia groups were set up and Laskar Jihad, a group of militant Islamic fundamentalists allied to the Indonesian army, was now moving into the province. Leaders were tailed and monitored and death lists drawn up. Then, on the night of 11 November 2001, on his way back from a dinner in the capital with members of Indonesia's special forces, West Papua's most prominent pro-independence leader, Theys Eluay, was murdered.

It was a deliberate assassination designed to divide the independence movement and provoke the Papuans to violence. When riots broke out in Sentani, Theys' home town, it looked for a moment as if the strategy might work. But the West Papuan leaders called for calm and the people, for the moment, kept their heads.

I went to West Papua in April 2002 to explore the aftermath of the Eluay assassination and to have a look at the independence movement on the ground. West Papua is remote and expensive to travel to. These reasons alone are enough to deter most visitors, but the Indonesian military has until recently made it doubly difficult for journalists to spend any amount of time there. It is commonplace for journalists requesting visas to travel to Papua to have their request denied with little or no reason given. To travel there "undercover" as a tourist is to risk arrest, and this has, in fact, become increasingly common. On arrival the journalist is heavily monitored, he is kept track of and the atmosphere of intimidation and subtle threat from the Indonesian authorities makes West Papua a very unpleasant place to work. But the threats to foreigners are negligible compared to the risks incurred by those people – leaders, activists, human rights workers – who persist in trying to maintain a flow of reliable information from the province regarding the activities of the Indonesian authorities who are engaged in the business of repressing them. Because of this climate of fear inside West Papua and the effect it has on what people will say, I knew I also needed to speak to the guerrilla leaders of the OPM (the Free Papua Movement), which has long been the umbrella group for the resistance to Indonesian occupation.

In July 2002 I travelled to Vanimo in Papua New Guinea, just across the border from West Papua, to interview Mathias Wenda, the commander of the arms-bearing division of the OPM known as the OPM–TPN or the Liberation Army of West Papua.

The guerrillas Wenda commands are the inheritors of an armed struggle that began almost as soon as the Indonesians arrived. In 1963, a broad-based resistance led to uprisings in several regions of West Papua before the Act of Free Choice. Then, in 1977, revolt in Wamena in the highlands spread to almost all the regions of the province.

Many of those now in the camps on both sides of the border, training as soldiers and pledging allegiance to the OPM, are highlanders. Some like Wenda fled in the late seventies and early eighties as the operations against them intensified. Others took flight more recently. For these guerrillas, the death of Theys was a call to arms. The non-violent dialogue he had espoused had only led to his death.

The repressive strategy being played out now in West Papua by the Indonesian authorities is an intimately familiar one. Only the most blinkered and partisan supporter of Jakarta could refuse to admit to the culpability of the Indonesian military in the destruction of East Timor in 1999, an event that forced the Australian government in the end to act decisively to stop the violence under massive Australian public pressure. Now, as the same Indonesian commanders and the same instrumentalities of its military elite are moving towards a comparable goal in a province that also lies directly to the north of Australia, the line has been drawn and it seems we have no outrage left.

I wasn't prepared for Vanimo to be so much like northern Australia. Aluminium houses on stilts with cyclone fences, Steve Liebmann and *Today* on the only television channel every morning, football commentaries blaring out of every house and a Westpac Bank that reminded me of one in Tennant Creek. Vanimo had the same functional architecture of warehouses and workshops with walls of pressed green tin and air-conditioned offices made from converted shipping containers. The food at the takeaway shop – meat pies, chips and fried chicken – was the same as at any lunch shop back in Australia, complete with a greasy bain-marie. The State of Origin rugby final between Queensland and New South Wales had been on the night before and the soldiers from the local Papua New Guinea Defence Force (PNGDF) detachment were nursing hangovers, and so I imagine was the PNG foreign affairs representative who had begun drinking yesterday morning in preparation for the big match. He had joined me for lunch on that day, accompanied by the man he introduced as the head of military intelligence for the PNG–Indonesia border.

Although part of Papua New Guinea, Vanimo is only thirty kilometres from Indonesia and forty kilometres from the capital of West Papua, Jayapura. As the only sizeable town on the northern tip of the PNG mainland, it has always been the first port of call for those fleeing the Indonesian military on the other side of the border. The first major wave of refugees arrived in 1969 after the UN-sponsored Act of Free Choice. In the lead-up to the Act, two West Papuan leaders stopped over in Vanimo en-route to New York to complain about the way the vote was being conducted. The Australian authorities detained them and flew them instead to Manus Island (where Howard put the people from the *Tampa*), from where their complaints to New York were never heard.

Little has changed since then. For the PNG government, everything to do with the border is an annoyance, something to be ignored or played down. Its stance is in line with the longstanding Australian policy of pretending nothing untoward happens inside Indonesia's easternmost province; as most PNG citizens will tell you, the money (A$323.7 million in 2000–2001) Australia gives its former colony each year ensures they effectively have no foreign policy independent of Australia. Now there are only 150 PNGDF troops stationed in Vanimo. It was early in the day when their commanders joined me in one of the two bars in town to find out what I was doing there. As we talked, four soldiers – the commanders' entourage – sat at a separate table watching us.

"What we have here are criminal elements. Wave-riders and hangers-on. They are easily led," said the head of military intelligence, referring to the latest batch of border crossers now living outside of Vanimo. "We want to do patrols but we can't get the money. We could stop it very easily and send them back across. The recommendations for funds go down to Moresby but nothing ever happens. The bureaucracy there is too politicised." It was clear that the presence of the refugees from West Papua was a bad thing, a problem that should have been solved a long time ago. They were, in his eyes, stupid, murderous people who brought nothing but trouble. The border was peaceful. The Indonesian military had not carried out an incursion into PNG for seven years. There were no problems here. The 318 refugees outside the town stayed, in his opinion, only because of the free food they got from the church.

I told them I was headed for Jayapura, and the civilian head of foreign affairs told me he would take me to the border himself. He was already drunk at midday and had a pronounced nervous tick under one eye. He told me he had fought in Bougainville and the only thing he hated more than the Australian army was Australian journalists. "What are you doing here? You want to meet the OPM. I'll show you the OPM. They are criminals. They kidnap people." He told me that he and another of my lunch companions had helped resolve a recent OPM kidnapping: "We were both involved in the negotiations to release them. One time we had to go up there and stay in the bush. We shot a pig, drank beer, it was good fun – like a barbecue." He laughed and drank more beer and yelled at the waitress to bring him his food. He started talking about the women in Jayapura. About how expensive the beer was and asked where I was going to stay. I told him which hotel. "Ha! So you know Jayapura. When were you there? Show me your fucking passport. I knew you were a fucking journalist," he screamed. He seemed happy with himself, showing off in front of the others. The military intelligence chief didn't seem to care. He told me that relations were good with the Indonesians. A memorandum of understanding had formalised arrangements. As far as the OPM were concerned, he wished they had the means to arrest them all and that would be it, no more problem.

They told me to go get the Indonesian visa and they would take me to the border. I said I'd see them around and they laughed. "Of course you will, this is the only place we drink and don't worry, we know where you are."

Ten years before, in April 1992, a Swedish documentary film-maker, Per-Ove Carlsson, was found dead in a room in Kiunga, a village south of Vanimo and close to the border. Carlsson had travelled to the region to make a film about the OPM. Although the official version proclaimed that he had cut his throat with his own knife, the death was widely believed, according to the international Committee to Protect Journalists, to be a case of Indonesian-financed assassination.

Max Watts, a veteran European journalist based in Sydney, was given the job of following up the death for the Swedish newspaper *Aftonbladet*. Watts established that a ragged, tired and broke Carlsson had returned from a two-week trip to see the OPM near Kiunga. Asking a local French-speaking Catholic priest about where to stay, he was directed to the house of a local schoolteacher. He went to bed early in the only upstairs room and in the morning, according to the schoolteacher, blood dripping through the ceiling alerted him and his family to the fact that something was wrong. The schoolteacher said the room was locked from the inside and Carlsson was dead with a fourteen-centimetre cut to his throat that had been administered with the saw blade of his Swiss army knife. Watts recalls asking a doctor if it was possible to commit suicide in such a way. He was told that it was in theory, but it was probably the most painful drawn-out way to cut one's throat. Why, for instance, didn't he use the standard blade?

When Watts tried to follow up on the story by phone from Australia, he met dead ends: "The schoolteacher left town unexpectedly very shortly after and the whole matter was closed. From what I could work out, if it wasn't suicide then whoever had killed Carlsson had told the local people not to talk and had the power to enforce it." The PNG authorities said the matter was closed and were backed up by the Australian high commissioner in Port Moresby. On the day of his death, Carlsson had called a colleague in Sweden, Mats Brolin, who said, "He was very afraid that [his phone] was being tapped by the local police, and that he was being followed." Brolin also said that Carlsson was being monitored by Indonesian agents. Watts believes that the PNG police or Indonesian agents colluding with the police killed Carlsson. Nine hours of footage he had taken of the OPM and the refugee camps was the only thing missing from his possessions.

The Australian journalist Andrew Kilvert has written of the close relations between the Papua New Guinean and Indonesian military forces based on the border. In early 2000, he detailed the rewards given to local PNGDF commanders, intelligence officers and two federal MPs in mid-1999 after a joint military operation to secure the release of five Indonesian hostages held by the OPM. According to Kilvert, the Indonesian military provided the group with a two-day stay in Jayapura along with thirty-five prostitutes and a large sum of US dollars. Later, the PNGDF commander-in-chief, Major-General Singirok, was also reportedly rewarded for his forces' involvement in the operation with a paid holiday to Biak Island for himself and his family. From what my companions had said at lunch, it was clear that they had been among the recipients of this Indonesian largesse.

In Vanimo that night I was reminded of the Carlsson story enough to put the spare bed in the hotel room against the door. But I needn't have bothered. The whole town, it seemed, was watching the State of Origin game.

"If you're not back by five tomorrow, I'm not waiting," the driver said. He realised now that I wasn't just getting a ride to the border and that the West Papuans with me in the car were there for a reason. There are not a lot of reasons to be in Vanimo unless you want to cross the border to Jayapura or visit the OPM camps just inside PNG. I'd told the fellow from military intelligence and the foreign affairs man that I would make my own way and they had lost interest long enough for me to get away.

On the way up to the border the driver had talked freely about how one day they could pull it down and just let the people cross. "We are the same people," he had said. It was a view held by many Papua New Guineans. There was no difference between the people of West Papua and those of PNG; only history and colonialism and now the poverty of those in the West made them different. "Look, what can I do? They are human beings as well," he had said, making room in the back for two more of the West Papuans who wanted to accompany me to the camp. The fact that Australia had made the border and imposed its policies on the PNG government also grated on him, and he started talking about how PNG was still not really independent from its former colonial boss. But he didn't want to hang around once he knew who I was going to meet.

Away from the road it was immediately thick jungle. The trees rose straight up two to three hundred feet above and the bush and ferns came up over head height. The path was a combination of mud and logs thrown over thick thorn bushes and gullies, and the five men walked with me in silence across the slimy logs balancing supplies of rice, kerosene and a typewriter on their heads. By the time we got to a small clearing, I was glad to stop and the leader, Peter, told us to wait for the guards. No sooner had he spoken than a man with a thick black beard dressed in ragged shorts and a singlet and carrying a machete came out of the scrub, walked up to Peter, drew himself rigidly to attention and boomed "*Siap*" – Indonesian for "Ready". Everybody dropped what they were carrying and stood to attention.

To make the camp they had felled two or three of the enormous trees we had been walking among. Five long huts on stilts served as the head-quarters. They had only been in the camp a few weeks and it had not yet been discovered by either the Indonesians or the PNGDF. A parade ground with a flagpole was situated in the middle and five men armed with an M-16, an AK-47 and some shotguns and a bolt-action rifle presented arms as we came in sweating from the bush. Others stopped work on construct-ing the camp to watch the spectacle. The leader, Mathias Wenda, Supreme Commander of the Liberation Army of West Papua, was in the hut behind and we walked in and sat cross-legged on the rough plank floor.

After the barest of introductions he wanted to start, and when I put my tape recorder in front of him he began speaking in a loud voice. He was addressing everyone in the low-roofed, rough wooden hut. There would have been about thirty who crowded in after us. His small, tightly muscled body coiling up with the effort of talking, he proclaimed his story to the whole camp. "I have been fighting since 1969. I have been here for twenty-two years continuing the struggle on the border. Since 1969 we have been fighting. Every day, every month, every year we have been fighting for independence." He raised his voice even louder, yelling in Indonesian at the top of his voice, "With the reporter coming from Australia the people of Papua want our desire for independence broadcast in radio, press and TV. We reject autonomy. We want full independence ... People have helped East Timor and Aceh whereas the people of West Papua have not got any help ... East Timor did not have few victims but in Papua there have been thousands. There have been so many victims in West Papua, and America and Australia don't see it ... because they are wearing Indonesian glasses. There is gold here and they are taking the profits of the land so both Australia and the United States defend Indonesia! But God has given me

Papua so I will defend it!" He paused and glared in my direction as if to say "Enough for the moment."

Mathias says the last time he and his men did any fighting was on 8 December 2000, when they killed nine Indonesian soldiers on the border. His men had just one automatic weapon, together with knives, bows and arrows; and, according to him, they hunted down the soldiers one by one. The deaths of these Indonesians were never reported, because, he says, "These things never are reported by Indonesia."

The fighting followed an OPM attack the previous day on a police station in the town of Abepura, the home of West Papua's main university. An Indonesian police officer was killed in the attack and the Indonesian police went on a rampage, beating and detaining anybody they suspected of being linked to the attack. Hundreds of young people fled Abepura for the border where Mathias's men attacked the Indonesians to cause a diversion. What had precipitated the attack on the police station in the first place was the cutting down of the West Papuan Morning Star flag by the Indonesian authorities in the centre of Jayapura. It had been openly flown in Jayapura and Abepura since the Second Papuan Congress in June 2000, and it stood as a symbol of hope and resistance in the wake of the congress's call for independence. "In 2000 all of the West Papuans, particularly those in the highlands, they all want independence and demonstrated and went to the congress in Jayapura," says Mathias, with the air of one whose worst fears are confirmed. "We stay here maintaining this position but now they come here as refugees. Their people were killed by the police and now they come to me here." The influx of people across the border peaked at about a thousand early in 2001 as people fled the long-expected crackdown on the independence movement. Many of the younger fighters now in Wenda's camp joined him at that time.

On 23 January 2001, Wenda and twelve of his men were arrested by the PNG police for being on PNG territory illegally, and charged with setting up and training an illegal army. It was a sign that the PNG authorities in Vanimo had moved from their former ambiguously neutral position toward the OPM. Now, because of the renewed activity on the border, the Indonesians had used their influence with the local PNG authorities to have the OPM leader arrested. Despite calls from the new Indonesian police chief in Jayapura, Made Pastika, to deport Wenda to Indonesia, he was quietly released after four months and made his way back to the bush.

When I ask him about why he was arrested, Wenda becomes vocal and furious. He rails against the Indonesians and against the United Nations for allowing the Act of Free Choice to go through. Against Australia for doing nothing all these years and not acknowledging the killing, past and present, that is being done by the Indonesian military in West Papua, and against the United States for making money out of West Papua. He focuses on the intimidation of the West Papuan people: "The people want to support the sovereignty of West Papua, but the military go to them with guns and they are frightened ... The same happened in 1969. When the UN came here, we wanted to ask for independence for West Papua. I was one of the members [of the OPM] in 1969 so they went *tek tek*," he says, making a shooting gesture at those around him. "The same is happening now. They are using weapons against all Papuans who want independence. ... If we had weapons it would be war! war! war! Until the Papuan people are free or annihilated." That's it. He is sick of the interview now. He leans over to his men and says, "I don't believe in him. The journalists, they just keep talking about the problem. The journalists just go away again. If we had weapons we could boil the Indonesians. They would go if the Papuans ran amok. I say look with your eyes. We could talk if you help us. We could work together. But they just talk."

A large wooden bowl of sago is brought into the hut. It is basically a pale pink, translucent lump of goo that is made by mixing and beating the inside of the sago palm. It has barely any nutritional value but it is full of starch and it does fill you up. The men sit around the bowl and say a quick prayer and then eagerly scoop up slabs of the sago with a large two-pronged wooden fork and place it on wooden plates. Some boiled leaves are added and that is the staple meal in the border camps.

Peter Tabuni has been with Mathias Wenda since the war started in their area of the Baliem Valley around Wamena in 1969. We are sitting cross-legged on the floor of one of the smaller wooden huts where your head almost touches the ceiling. It is dark now and the only light comes from a small kerosene lamp. Aside from the lamp there is no other furnishing. "Now I want to talk about some people killed by soldiers in 1969, 1977 and 1984. I am the only witness to this story," he begins. "Mr Wenda, I work for him. He has followed the struggle since he was nineteen years old. We follow the OPM. I haven't even got a beard yet. The first killings happen in 1969 about the Act of Free Choice. Indonesia like to give auton-omy status for us. They use guns, they are stronger. Caution us to follow Act of Free Choice. Because they use the gun and talk strong to us we are angry so we kill two soldiers. They kill us – about 500 people – and we move and stay in the bush. We don't eat something when we live in the bush. We talk about independence but they want to harass and retaliate. They fight us because we do not agree with their program. This program for independence, they delay it then they report to the United Nations that we fight each other. They say we cannot govern ourselves. So the UN says the *Pepera* [Act of Free Choice] is true. But it is not what the people want. Indonesia is stronger. After free choice we go back to the village. They take some of our women and girls and our pigs. They were not good to us so we are against them. We grow our thing for independence so at that time all the people from Wamena decide to fight the Indonesians. It starts on 24 April 1977. The problems grow again with Indonesia. At that time in 1977, 1978, 1979, 1,179 people were killed. From 1980 to 1983, 2,126. 1984 to 1990, 1,144. From 1991 to 1995, 672. From 1996 to 1999, 852. From 1999 to 2002, 535. That is only from Wamena, I don't count the other ten provinces," he says. I ask him where he got the figures from and he hands me a very dirty cardboard-covered journal. Inside in tiny hand-writing on yellowing water-stained paper are recorded the names and dates and details of each death. It is arranged in columns and logged in a way I can't really follow, like a complicated train timetable. "That is my document, how many killed in Wamena. From '77 until '84 I was there and I gathered the information myself but from '85 to 2002 I got the figures from other men who sent them to me here. Some of them were killed by Indonesia. Some of them die in the bush. They run away from Indonesia and they die in the bush, in the mountains, in the river. They walk to here." He pauses. "Their story is here in this document and I write only about what I know or I have seen," he says solemnly.

"When we go against Indonesia we do not use guns, we use traditional weapons. They use many kinds of weapons against us. Indonesians use murdering weapons against us like guns and helicopters or bombs. They want to finish us off."

He hands me another tattered yellowing document. This one is written in English and had been prepared by him for the UN decolonisation committee seminar held in Port Moresby in 1993. It lists individual instances of killing and torture by the Indonesian military against OPM members and civilians dating back to 1963 when the Indonesians first arrived and total estimates of Papuan deaths from Indonesian campaigns.

Some of the entries are worth quoting:

The Baliem insurgency (June 1977–December 1978): "Indonesian reinforcements flown in from Jayapura, Biak, Nabire and Ambon in Moluccas islands. The Villages of the Dani and general warrior tribes of Highlands retreated to the mountains armed with spears, bows and arrows. Thousands bravely challenged the Indonesian soldiers using traditional war tactics in the open field but easily machine-gunned down in the hundreds and thousands by Indonesian armed forces. Many villagers apprehended/arrested and in hundreds or in thousands were taken to the Baliem River where they were executed and thrown into the river. Some tens, hundreds and even thousands of men, women and children were forcefully taken into the church buildings and any other institutional buildings set up by the missionaries in the area, and burned. Either alive or after being shot dead along with those buildings and houses."

The report then ran through what happened in a few specific cases: "In one of the events in Kelila over one thousand people comprised of church leaders, community leaders, tribal chiefs and many other men old and young were forcefully gathered and forced into a clinic hall (too many the people could not move) the soldiers then machine-gunned through the house and then set them on fire. The half-burned people were then pulled out and dumped into a mass grave which was dug up later."

It detailed the deaths of OPM leaders in the operation. 1977, Piramid: "Carlos Pagawak, the deputy commander of the OPM region II command was arrested. He was tortured to dead by using heated hot iron rod. Before being tortured he was chained then hot iron was used to push into his left eye, his nose, then to his sides and anus. Carlos Pagawak died of that torture."

In the same area in 1977: "The wife of Mathias Wenda (Commander OPM) was arrested ... when she admitted she had no knowledge of her husband's whereabouts, she was forcefully taken to the soldiers' base. There her legs and hands were tightened apart and she was repeatedly raped, one after the other by about forty-two soldiers for one whole day until she was almost dead."

1977, Tiom: "A local Pastor of the Lutheran Evangelical Church, Rev Turangen Wenda, was arrested. He was arrested and went through heavy interrogation, then tortured with a heated iron rod. Pushing through his eyes, nose, anus and piercing through his sides, killing him."

1978, Agandugume: "A pregnant women by the name of Kindega Murip was shot and killed. Her belly was slashed open by bayonet. The baby in the womb was also killed by the bayonet cut. The soldiers pull out the baby from the womb and in the place filled in with English cabbage and other greens they could get hold of near the scene."

The report stated that, according to OPM records, 84,000 people died in the 1977–78 operation throughout the regions of Timika, Wamena and Fak Fak – almost all of West Papua except for the northern coast.

Pages of detailed gruesome information followed. In broken English it ran through deaths by torture, incidents of mass killing, rapes and the deaths of OPM leaders. The last entry related to the killing of one OPM leader, Martin Luther Prawar, on 31 May 1992 after he had returned secretly to Jayapura from the border.

Peter stared at me as I read it. I got the feeling that he alone out of those in the camp felt that this was valuable. Nobody else I had asked seemed the slightest bit interested in recounting in detail any events that had occurred more than a year ago. The report was incomplete and hard to understand but it gave a glimpse of what had happened to these people to bring them here. "They don't just kill with the gun. One man I saw still alive they burnt his head and feet and they wire his hands together and cook him over a fire and then they put a hot iron over his body. They cut the hand and ear of some and cook it on the fire and give it to them to eat. Some of them they wire their hands and put them in the field and shoot. I am eyewitness to this myself in '77, '78, '79 in Tiam district in Wamena. I forgot one time they put a stick in a man's anus and it comes out his mouth and he died," he continued. He had a whole lifetime of grisly stories.

"Many people from West Papua, many more they are killed, but Indonesia they close it and they say to other countries it is a small problem. We are men but they kill us like animals but other countries are not talking about it."

Mathias Wenda came in to the hut. He motioned Peter to be quiet. Peter started gathering up the documents and Mathias sat down in front of me and stared directly at me. "Now we are alone we can talk in private," he said. He began with a question: "Is there something you have come here to tell me?" I said no, that I had just come to report what he and his men were doing, how the movement was going, what their plans were, that kind of thing. He looked annoyed. "Who sent you? Is it about the weapons? We can talk privately now? Are you here to help us?" I felt uneasy. No one had sent me. I hadn't even really got permission from the OPM leadership abroad to come here. I rolled a cigarette and offered the tobacco around but no one took it this time. They were all staring, waiting for an answer. It felt like an interrogation and I thought I had better verify my credentials. I started by telling him how I had met his "spokesman" in Jayapura two months before. How he had relayed a faxed message from the commander containing his statement on the resumption of armed resistance to the Indonesians following the death of Papuan Presidium Council leader Theys Eluay last November. I told him how the spokesman had explained to me about the weapons the OPM had acquired in PNG and how they were now conducting training. He had told me how the OPM were paying Chinese and Malaysian businessmen between 7,000 and 5,000 PNG kina (A$3,500 and $2,500) for each weapon, depending on the condition. Wenda's eyes widened when what I said was translated back to him. Yes, he had sent the fax and yes, they were conducting training but, "As you can see I only have five guns," he said angrily. I couldn't tell whether he was angry with me or angry with his subordinate in Jayapura for telling me too much or whether he felt I was some kind of spy and he had to deny everything.

He started talking about weapons; how to get them, what he needed, where they could be bought, how much they would cost. I had to say over and over that I was a journalist and it wasn't my role to supply him with weapons. I was aware of the problem he had and all I could do was report it. It has been the fundamental problem of the OPM since they began. Aside from a small quantity of weapons captured from the Indonesians, they have received no support from the outside world since they began their struggle in the early sixties. The land border to PNG was Australia's responsibility until independence in 1975 and, as a US ally and a diplomatic supporter of Indonesian rule in West Papua, Australia has done everything it can to ensure that the OPM remains hopelessly under-armed in its struggle against the might of Indonesia's internationally trained and armed military. Since PNG achieved independence, the PNGDF, trained by (and up until the early eighties staffed by officers of) the Australian army, has maintained the blockade against the OPM.

Australian journalist Ben Bohane, who in 1995 was the first journalist to visit the OPM inside West Papua, has visited three of the main OPM command areas since. He estimates that the OPM has between 300 to 500 weapons with no sophisticated network to obtain more. "Most would be captured from ambushes with Indo troops, some would have actually been sold by Indo troops, some have come up through Torres Strait (the preferred supply route from Australia) and some have been guns-for-ganja swaps with PNG raskol gangs or international criminal groups," he says.

My conversation with Wenda went round in circles. There was no way that I could possibly get him weapons, even if I wanted to, but that wasn't the response he was after. I got the feeling that my visit was being interpreted as the long-awaited sign that things were going to change. That help was on its way. That finally they were going to get what they needed to defeat the Indonesians. He kept talking and I didn't dare to interrupt him or contradict him. I had seen the flash of violence in his eyes when I asked him about the weapons and I didn't want to see it again. The long day, the heat and the tension were all starting to get the better of me and I began to have trouble keeping my eyes open and stopping myself from yawning. He called it a night and left in disappointment to sleep at the other end of the hut, and I just lay down where I had been sitting and fell asleep.

On the next day I woke to a rehearsal parade and raising of the Morning Star flag to commemorate the anniversary of West Papuan independence. It was on 1 July 1971 that a group of West Papuan OPM leaders announced the independence of West Papua in the capital Jayapura, using the Papuan name for the city, Port Numbay. The declaration was born of frustration with the UN's failure to respond to the protests they had made regarding the conduct of the 1969 Act of Free Choice. It passed barely noticed in the outside world with the only consequence of the proclamation being an increase in Indonesian operations against the OPM.

Two hundred and forty fighters have gathered in the camp to begin another round of training. Wenda takes the opportunity to hand out newly arrived shoulder boards to his staff. They affix them to their military-style shirts. Some of them have the basic green Indonesian civil service shirts, others have the Indonesian army camouflage and Wenda himself puts on an old oversized Australian Army dress tunic with the new shoulder boards that give him the rank of general.

They have nine regional commanders, they explain, and a general staff which is here at the camp. The other commanders are based in every region of West Papua all the way to Sorong at the western tip. Mathias says each regional commander controls five "battalions" of 400 to 500 people each. That means roughly 20,000 Liberation Army members throughout West Papua together with those on the border.

The flag-raising ceremony is simple and grave. The two hundred or so troops line up in formation and march into the clearing under the direction of an officer. Most have only spears, bows and arrows or sticks and they present arms with these. The men with the automatic weapons form an honour guard for the flag. Unlike the others they have full camouflage uniforms. The flag is raised, the proclamation of independence is read and the national anthem sung. Some of them have tears in their eyes as they hold the salute to the flag while they sing. They stand so long in the sun listening to the speech of their commander that one of them faints and is quietly carried away. Afterwards they continue drilling for at least two hours, stamping back and forth across the clearing in bare feet.

Back in Vanimo, as I wait in the small airport for the afternoon flight to Moresby, an old Papuan man approaches and introduces himself. His name is Nicholas Nere, and he is a West Papuan who has lived in Vanimo since 1965 when he fled Jayapura after being jailed by the Indonesians for political activity. Understanding that they would eventually have to leave, the Dutch embarked on an educational program in the fifties to prepare the West Papuans to govern themselves rather than become a part of Indonesia. Nere had been a member of this newly created West Papuan Dutch-educated elite.

History made the Dutch promise a hollow one. From 1954 onwards Indonesia's first president, Sukarno, laid claim to West Papua: all that had been the Dutch East Indies was now to be Indonesia. The Dutch felt otherwise and remained in what they called West New Guinea on the grounds that the people were of a different race, being Melanesian and not Malay or Asian, and the claim of the newly independent Indonesia was therefore baseless. The unspoken element in the argument was the mineral resources of West Papua and who would later have the right to exploit them, but at the time the public argument was a racial one.

Indonesia pressed its claim by dropping paratroopers in remote parts of the territory and threatening a naval blockade and outright war against the Dutch. Cold War politics intervened and US President John F. Kennedy, fearful of Soviet bloc influence with Indonesia and keen to curry favour with Sukarno, pressured Holland to relinquish its claim, which it eventually did in the New York Agreement of 1962. A United Nations transitional authority, UNTEA, was set up to oversee the transfer of administration from the Dutch to the Indonesians. Behind all of this was the then un-published knowledge of the mountain of gold that would become the Freeport mine. Both the Dutch and the Americans knew of the mineral wealth that waited for exploitation in West Papua but neither referred to it directly. Australia, although it had proposed an eventual union between its colony of Papua New Guinea and the Dutch territory, fell into line with American policy and withdrew its diplomatic support for the Dutch position.

For Nere, the whole experience was a bitter one. In 1961, when he was studying in Holland, the Dutch had promised independence for the colony by 1971. He remembers reading the details of the proposal in the government gazette. When he returned in 1962, he was assigned to work with the United Nations transitional authority to facilitate the handover. He says he remembers working on this mission with a young Kofi Annan who, according to Nere, "supported the Muslims" (the Indonesians). "At the time I was working with the United Nations and we hand over to the

Indonesians on 1 May 1963. Then they arrest me and put me in prison for two years as a political prisoner. I'm supposed to be carrying out the New York Agreement. In that agreement there are articles 18 to 22 regarding the right of self-determination for the people of West Papua and then they change it to Indonesian rule and the Act of Free Choice. The right of self-determination is one man one vote, not a consultative system. What they did was without the consensus of the Papuan people." Nere is referring to the voting system that allowed Indonesia to select a tiny proportion of the Papuan population as representatives to confirm Indonesia's claim on the province.

After he was released from jail in 1965 Nere was put under house arrest in Jayapura. His response was to flee to Vanimo and, as a citizen of the Netherlands, apply for political asylum in Australia. But the Australian authorities blocked his application and instead he found himself working for the Australian administration and became a PNG citizen. In 1995 he was awarded an OBE for his services in PNG. Now that he is retired he says he wants to speak out about the problem because he was told by the Australian authorities to keep quiet because of his work. According to Nere, the UN washed its hands of West Papua: "In 1969 they conducted the Act of Free Choice. The New York Agreement said one way but they conducted it in a different way, the Indonesian way – we don't want that. This means the United Nations are bullshitting us. And our property and our common dignity that God created for us is given away."

In 2001 an Associated Press reporter in Jakarta, Slobodan Lekic, spoke to one of the UN staffers who was instrumental in organising the Act of Free Choice. "It was just a whitewash. The mood at the United Nations was to get rid of this problem as quickly as possible," Chakravarthy Narasimhan, a retired UN undersecretary general, told Lekic from his home in Madras, India, where he is now retired. "Nobody gave a thought to the fact that there were a million people there who had their fundamental human rights trampled," he told Lekic, breaking the long silence maintained by UN officials involved in the ballot.

Nicholas Nere says 28,000 West Papuans crossed the border following the Act of Free Choice and they have continued coming ever since. In 1971 they came after the OPM declaration of independence, in 1977 and 1978 following the uprisings in Baliem Valley. In 1984 the provocation was the desertion of Papuans in the Indonesian army and the killing of the leader Arnold Ap, in 1996 border crossings were sparked off by the reprisals after the OPM hostage taking in Mapnduma and in late 2000 they followed in the wake of the Abepura police station attack and the inevitable reprisals. "We ask the United Nations to come back on that case again and have a look at that one. If no, we can take it to an international court to condemn this national disaster. We have no guns but we can't win with guns. We don't want that. We have to have the UN back."

OPM-TPN Supreme Commander Mathias Wenda (left) with senior commanders.

OPM fighters at Wenda's border camp.

Indonesian troops jog past Theys Eluay's house in Sentani.

"WE WILL DIE ALONE"

The burnt-out shells of buildings, devastated in the riot that broke out after the death of the leader Theys Eluay, line the road from the airport. Small stalls, selling the usual Indonesian staples of clove cigarettes, individually or in packets, instant noodles and bottled water, adjoin local Papuans selling betel nut and lime in the shade thrown by the burnt-out buildings. Across the road from the house of the former leader, a group of young Papuan men sit on the curb, chew betel nut and say they are defending the leader's house and his grave which is across the road in the football field.

It is six months since the leader was found dead in his car, apparently strangled or suffocated with a plastic bag after he had attended a dinner with Kopassus (Indonesia's notorious special force troops) and senior Indonesian military in nearby Jayapura. The only witness, his driver, has not been seen since and is thought to have been killed by the same people who carried out the murder. The Indonesian investigation has concluded that it was a Kopassus killing and has charged three officers and seven subordinates, but they have not been brought to trial and with a lack of witnesses the case looks shaky. Over the last six months, the Indonesian authorities have bit by bit had to admit what everybody else here assumed when Theys' body was discovered in his car lodged halfway down a ravine on 11 November 2001: that he was killed by Kopassus because he was a leader who proposed independence for West Papua.

Theys didn't come to the fore as an independence leader until late 1998, when the fall of Suharto sparked calls for change and there were challenges across Indonesia to the repressive power of the military. Before then he was a member of the local parliament and a member of Suharto's Golkar Party. In 1969 he was one of the leaders who signed the Act of Free Choice and it was said he aided the Indonesians in identifying those Papuans in his area of Sentani who still had sympathies for the Dutch and for independence. Then, as a member of the Indonesian-sponsored council of traditional leaders – the *Adat* council – Theys start-ed to become a focus for pro-independence sentiment. He was one of a hundred leaders who went to Jakarta in January 1999 to ask President Habibie for West Papua's independence.

By the time of the first Papua Congress in February 2000, Theys was the most popular leader among the mostly Indonesian-employed and educated Papuan elite. As a traditional leader in Sentani, he also had the support of the traditional chiefs throughout West Papua. On top of that he was the leader of *Satgas Papua* (Papua Taskforce) a 5,000-strong force of pro-independence young people who provided security for the congress. It was a heady time. Theys Eluay provided a bridge between the tribal leaders, the urban elite and the OPM-TPN fighters still in the bush. The Papuan Morning Star flag was flown publicly, Indonesian reprisals were not immediate and many believed independence was finally on its way. At the Second Papuan Congress in Jayapura in May and June 2000, Theys pro-claimed himself chairman of the thirty-one member Papuan Presidium Council that the congress elected to represent the West Papuan people in their struggle for independence. The council pledged to pursue this goal in a non-violent way and to pressure Jakarta for a referendum.

Theys was not without his critics. Through this time there were also mutterings about his good relations with the Indonesian military, and about the role of *Satgas Papua* led by his son, Boy Eluay. It was noted that Theys took money from the military and from the Wahid government, which provided funding to the Presidium Council.

Even so, with his wild shock of white hair and penchant for loud gaudy shirts, and his lack of reverence for authority, Theys connected with ordinary Papuans. Maybe as he became more popular with the people he just loved the attention and started to make bolder and more public demands for independence. He spoke of peace and prayer as the means by which the West Papuan people would achieve this. He became so popular that the military must have decided he was dangerous and they invited him to dinner at the Hamadi barracks in Jayapura to celebrate

Heroes Day – a commemoration of those who fought against the Dutch for independence. On the way home on 11 November 2001, the car was stopped on a lonely part of the road. His driver made a frantic mobile call and was cut off. The next day Theys' body was found. The only other witness to the killing, his driver, is still missing.

His supporters in Sentani responded by burning down the main street. Shops, banks and a hotel were destroyed. The army was deployed in huge numbers. Sentani is the site of the province's main airport and an important transport hub. The Papuan leaders appealed for calm. Theys' funeral was attended by tens of thousands of people. By killing him the Indonesian military had wiped away the stain of his association with them and he was more popular than he had ever been before. But his death also threw the new pro-independence elite into paralysis. Many believed the death of Theys was the beginning of a program by the Indonesian military to wipe out the independence movement. A plan of action to this effect and a list with Theys' name on the top was widely circulated and the movement received a setback from which it hasn't yet recovered.

When I went to the house to see Boy Eluay to ask about his father's death, a red-eyed, swaying Papuan with a black t-shirt told me to get out. Boy was sick with malaria and didn't want to see any more journalists. Outside, a column of TNI troops jogged past on the main street chanting. The young men chewing betel nut just sat back and rolled their eyes at the daily show of strength and didn't move from their place opposite the dead leader's house.

As vice-chairman of the Presidium Council, Thom Beanal is now in charge, although he refuses to be called chairman until the death of his predecessor is fully investigated. He is a traditional leader of the Amungme people who own the land where Freeport, one of the largest gold and copper mines in the world, operates. He took the company to court in 1997 on behalf of his people for environmental and human rights abuses.

Freeport responded by employing him in early 2000 as a commissioner and contributing to the expenses of the Presidium, including the luxury, top-floor hotel suite with the sweeping views over Jayapura's harbour where I met him. Beanal is a big, heavy man with a thoughtful manner, who pauses professionally in the midst of his speech like a politician to search for the right word. His commanding presence, his deep voice coming from the back of his throat and his heavily jowled neck give him an air of authority that would not be out of place in a corporate boardroom. It is easy to see why he is a man whom Freeport feels it can deal with. Many saw Beanal's appointment as commissioner as a cynical manoeuvre by the US-based company to hedge its bets against the Indonesians by supporting the West Papuan independence movement in theory while continuing to profit hugely from its own sweetheart deal with the Indonesians.

Beanal's leadership style contrasts with the flamboyance of his predecessor. In simple terms, Theys was a big personality and his death has left a vacuum at the top of the Presidium Council. That the leader of the Presidium could be killed so openly was an obvious challenge to the authority of that body, and student groups and grass roots organisations like Demmak (a highlanders' association) have now begun to question the council's authority. For the OPM-TPN hardheads in the bush, Theys' death has undermined the credibility of peaceful dialogue as a way forward. What they say quite simply is "Where did it get him?" This is precisely what the Indonesian authorities were after: to split and destabilise the West Papuan push for independence.

The Presidium Council is for peaceful change and the only way Beanal sees that happening is by a referendum. He talks about a referendum this year or next but says, "We don't want it to be like East Timor. Them coming in and shooting people. That's what we are afraid of. If it [the referendum] were to happen, I would ask the UN to send soldiers. And first of all the army would have to go. If we do a referendum with the soldiers here, it will be like 1969 all over again." He is balancing between a public support base that is demanding some kind of action for independence and the Indonesian government who he admits is not listening. "There's no thought, they don't think, they don't speak with us. We talk about dialogue and it's as if they don't want to listen." The Presidium has forwarded proposals for a referendum to the UN and the Indonesians but they have received no reply.

"The UN should come here. They have a responsibility. The Papuans are just dying off and I feel the fault is with the UN. If there is time for talking, we could explain. In fact, with the problem of Papua, the Netherlands, Indonesia and the United States all have responsibility. We are being killed because of their mistakes." When I ask if the West Papuans have anybody lobbying the UN to return, Beanal says yes. They have one man, Otto Mota, a former journalist who is studying in New York but he doesn't have much money and can only lobby part-time.

The current Indonesian position is that they have made, in their own eyes, a very generous offer of special autonomy that is now being implemented. As well as a change of name for the province from "Irian Jaya" to "Papua" that took effect on 1 January 2002, it includes provision for 80 per cent of the revenue from West Papua to be redirected back to the province where it is to be dispersed at the discretion of the local legislature. The obvious shortcoming of this plan is that the legislature is still dominated by non-Papuans. Nevertheless, its proponents say that autonomy in regional spending and decision-making will eventually lead to administrative and institutional development, in turn allowing the local government to remedy the social problem of Papuans disadvantaged by Indonesia's economic domination.

Opposition to the autonomy package has plagued the proposal from the outset. Chris Ballard, writing in *Melanesia in Review*, has identified the governor, members of the local and national legislatures, senior academics, bureaucrats and church leaders as supporters of the legislation. These are precisely the groups that stand to gain financially. In contrast, the general community is cynical about what seems to be a trade-off of its main demand for a referendum and for independence in return for the financial benefit of the privileged few.

Beanal is unequivocal about who killed his predecessor and why. "We can see from Indonesia there is a program to kill as many leaders as possible. They [the Indonesian military] are trying to provoke us to violence but we are going to stick to the peaceful way. It is only an attempt at provocation, to get a reaction, from the Papuan people to the fact that they killed Theys. Perhaps tomorrow they will kill me or kill another leader."

Beanal tells the story of how after Theys' death he attended a Regional Security Council meeting at which the Indonesian military commander, the governor, the foreign ministry, the head of the university and the provincial police chief of Jayapura were all present. He becomes animated as he tells the story and leans forward. He is miming the action of holding a document in his hand and then throwing it down on the coffee table in front of us. "I said, 'Indonesia has a plan.' I usually speak directly with the military commander so I said, 'Have you got this plan to kill us?'"

The document in question revealed at a meeting in Jakarta on 8 June 2000, senior officials of the TNI, the police and secret services drew up a ground-plan to undermine West Papua's independence movement by taking "preventative and repressive action" to divide, discredit and destroy the Presidium Council and the Papuan struggle. Although the document had been circulating in human rights and activist circles in Jakarta and Jayapura for some time, it was only when Theys was killed that the dire strategies it foreshadowed received coverage.

Beanal continues: "I said, 'You killed him, there's a document.' And the military commander said, 'No, there isn't.' So we photocopied it and handed it out. They said they would study it and look into it." Since then three officers and seven *Kopassus* privates have been charged with Theys' murder but none of them has yet gone to trial. The case is still the subject of controversy, with the military insisting the men must be brought before a court martial, not a civilian court.

In a paper-driven bureaucracy like the Indonesian one, documents that disclose funding or directives for government programs, even repressive ones, often fall into the wrong hands. Papuans in the civil service or liberal-minded Indonesians ensure that a steady stream of incriminating evidence finds its way into the hands of activists and journalists. But there seems to be another more insidious reason for this dissemination. It is almost as if the power of a document, a death list for example, is multiplied if its contents are known to those who are threatened by it. The knowledge of the proposed threat is often enough to coerce and terrify people into curtailing their pro-independence activities. This is a further level of psychological terror designed to repress and smother dissent. With a track record like the Indonesian military's, to threaten is often enough. They don't have to carry out the killing or the massacre because the fact of everybody knowing what they intend to do achieves the effect they desire.

Johannes Bonai, the director of the only human rights monitoring group in West Papua, ELS-HAM, calmly tells me he is also on the death list. "The information we get from a member of the military, so we have to take it seriously," he says. His group held a press conference at 10 a.m. on 11 February 2002 detailing their findings into the death of Theys and the direct links to *Kopassus*. By midday they had their first phone call from the military threatening the director and the supervisor. It hasn't really affected Bonai's work so far. He produces a document from among the papers in his small airless office in Abepura that outlines the Indonesian government's expenditure on militia in West Papua for the last two years. It details how each of West Papua's fifteen administrative regions is annually allotted 641 million rupiah (approximately A$130,000) – a total of 9,615 million rupiah (approximately A$2 million) per year beginning in January 2000 – to be distributed to militia groups whose stated aims are to provide information to the military regarding pro-independence groups, to defend West Papua as part of Indonesia and to disseminate propaganda through the media, door to door and through religious and cultural groups. The document originated in the office of the Secretary of Administration for the National Intelligence Agency (BIN).

"The Indonesian government are trying to break up the Papuan people," Bonai says. "Until now we don't know exactly what they have planned, but we know in Fak Fak [a West Papuan town], Laskar Jihad members join *Gerakan Merah Putih* [militia] members and *Kostrad* [Army strategic reserve troops] and police in attacking civilians' houses and burning them down."

In a working paper, "Indonesian Security Responses to Resurgent Papuan Separatism", published by the Australian National University's Strategic and Defence Studies Centre in July 2001, analyst Matt Davies found plenty of evidence of Indonesian government and military programs. Much of it was in Indonesia's own press, linking the Indonesian government and military to the funding and formation of militia groups in West Papua. In a revelation he says is comparable to the Genardi document that provided a blueprint for the Indonesian military's September 1999 scorched earth program in East Timor three months before it happened, Davies refers to "a classified document from DEPDAGRI [Departement Dalam Negeri or Home Affairs], undisputed by Indonesian government sources". This document (first uncovered by film-maker Mark Worth in late 2000) shows a breakdown of payments and indicates DEPDAGRI's responsibility for an underground intelligence campaign using pro-integrationist militia throughout West Papua.

Davies describes how a "crash funding" program in the pro-independence region of Wamena was channelled into integrationist militia groups there and how the cash also went to the military to disburse. He goes on, "But control and influence at senior levels is apparent. In mid-2000, some identified as involved in the quite large payments were Interim Governor Air Vice Marshal (retired) Musiran Darmosuwito and Kodam Trikora Commander Major-General Ingkiriwang," then respectively the governor and area military commander of West Papua. At this time a rash of media reports described the establishment of militia groups in West Papua but attention died off when the expected violence failed to occur.

Another later document uncovered by journalist Ian Timberlake in Jakarta shows how the operation works in practice. Dated 8 April 2002 and originating in the district military command for Wamena, Kodim 1702/Jayawijaya, it gives a list of eighty names of people described as farmers and is headed "List of Satgas Merah Putih candidates from Kodim 1702/Jayawijaya". It is signed by the Indonesian military commander for Wamena. It is in essence a list of recruits into the local pro-integrationist militia who have been earmarked for payment.

Davies points out that in West Papua, as opposed to East Timor in late 1998, there has been a greater effort to infiltrate and compromise and "turn" existing separatist groups. In other words, the money is being spent to buy off those involved in independence activities rather than to pay outsiders to attack them, at least for the time being. The emergence of the province-wide pro-independence militia, *Satgas Papua*, has been exploited by the Indonesian security forces who have allowed it to grow unchecked and in some cases funded its activities as part of a sophisticated counter-insurgency program. The security forces have used the 20,000-strong *Satgas Papua* organisation to identify clandestine independence networks and personalities and target them for a future crackdown, which has already begun.

Those who support independence have exposed themselves to repressive action by revealing themselves to the authorities. It's the same as in East Timor after the fall of Suharto, when the Timorese people openly began to call for independence. At least in East Timor, help from the international community did arrive in the form of the first UN mission and observers. In West Papua the increased openness has only brought another wave of repression.

In a small village on the outskirts of Jayapura the group of representatives from *Demmak*, the highlanders' organisation, sit cross-legged on the floor of a wooden hut and I am handed another document. This one names the thirteen senior Indonesian intelligence operatives in the Wamena region. It is dated 5 January 2002 from Jakarta and details the plan for *Organisasi Pelaksana*, an organisation of security officials charged with a program to eliminate pro-independence highlanders from the Dani tribe, the largest tribe in Wamena. "We don't know 100 per cent what this plan is but we know they make a program for the killing of the Dani people," says Ledekime Nenyagi. "We know seventy to eighty-five weapons have been handed out [to militia forces] in Wamena already," says another man. "We feel this year independence must come to us. This year if the Indonesians are still here they will kill us."

Six hundred people had fled this village the previous December after the incident at the Abepura police station that Mathias Wenda had mentioned. Being mostly from the highlands, all the villagers were suspect and 300 Indonesian military newly arrived from Java had visited the small village. The people fled across the border to Vanimo and hadn't come back yet, leaving most of the houses empty.

One of their leaders, Benny Wenda, was supposed to be there that day but he hadn't arrived. The Indonesian intelligence had been looking for him that morning and had turned up where he was staying at 10 a.m. He was finally arrested in June this year and charged with being involved in the Abepura incident and with possessing a PNG passport. He is now in custody in Jayapura.

A few days later I am back in the same village. There are more people here now and they are organising a demonstration for the next day to welcome Ralph Boyce, the first US Ambassador to Indonesia to visit Jayapura since anybody can remember.

In the highland way the people cram into one of the houses and everyone sits cross-legged on the floor waiting to speak in turn. One old man brandishing a spear begins to talk. "In August this year with arrow and gun I want to fight. This is not joking. I am serious. I want to fight. What I am planning is a program now and you should not ask too many questions. You will find out. I don't have any guns. My people are being killed. That is why I want to talk to you." While he's talking he has raised himself up and is standing over me with his spear and he is yelling. Then he starts to cry. "Which country will come and fight with me? Will die with me? No one. We will die alone." He stops and waves the spear accusingly in my face, tears streaming down his cheeks. He sits down and a tall, skinny man takes his place. "We are all from the Baliem Valley. We are rich people. We have gold. We have oil. It is all from us. Freeport company, that is all our gold. But I have been in the jungle across the border in Vanimo for sixteen years. Your government from Australia, many times they come and talk to us. But now we must see results. I am angry with the Australian government because they do nothing for us here and they help the Indonesians. Why doesn't Australia speak about what happens here?" He glares at me and returns to his place on the floor. The next few people all labour the same point. They are sick of talking, sick of negotiations. They want independence and a referendum. Now, this year. The US ambassador is coming to review the Indonesian autonomy program that is supposed to satisfy the Papuans' demands for independence by redirecting a larger proportion of the revenue from the province back into the local economy. But these people have already rejected it. They say that the 80 per cent of the province's revenue that is supposed to come back to the province will be absorbed by the corrupt administration.

As one old man from *Demmak* mutters when I ask him about the autonomy program and the visit of the US ambassador, "I don't need delegates. I have 16,000 people ready for fighting Indonesia in one hour. We stand by with nothing but arrows, not guns. Next year we all from Wamena need independence. They all get it wrong. We want independence."

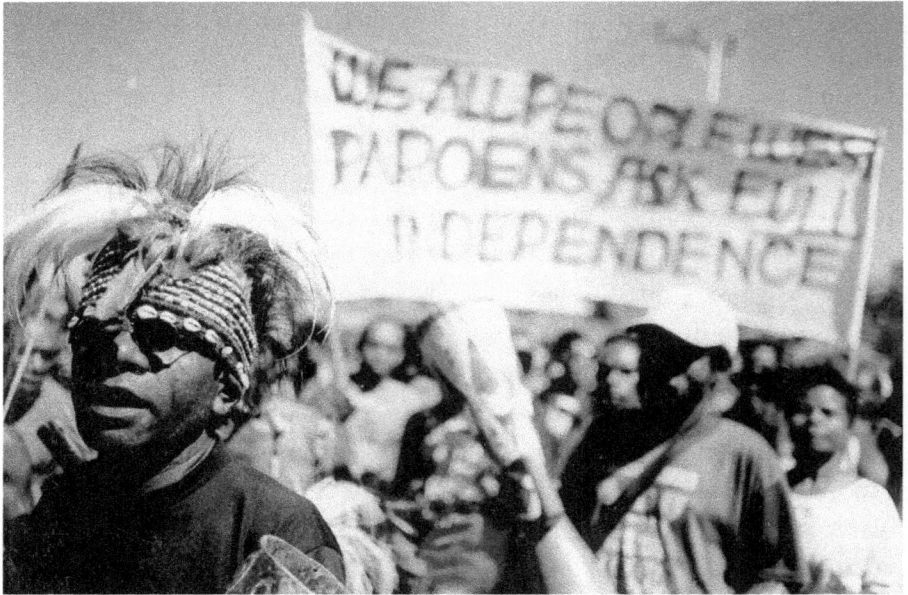

Pro-independence demonstration of 15 April to mark the arrival of US Ambassador Ralph Boyce in Sentani.

Dani warriors at the pro-independence demonstration.

THE EL DORADO OF CORRUPTION

Early on the morning of 15 April 2002 the US Ambassador to Indonesia, Ralph Boyce, arrived in Sentani airport with his entourage. He was greeted by almost a thousand pro-independence demonstrators. The demonstrators were mostly highlanders who, adorned in feathered head-dresses with some sporting the traditional penis gourds, danced and hustled the small US group up the road from the airport to the grave of Theys Eluay. It was a blindingly hot morning. The Ambassador and his press attaché were red in the face and dripping with sweat by the time I caught up with them as they listened to a short speech at Theys' grave from Presidium leader Thom Beanal. He presented them with a string bag and declared that the visit showed the full recognition West Papua now received from the outside world. The crowd, many holding Morning Star flags and banners rejecting autonomy, whooped with joy at the speech. The Ambassador looked annoyed. The whole thing wasn't on the agenda and he felt his presence was sending the wrong message. Along the street a group of Dani warriors made their characteristic spine-chilling, siren-like war whoop as they advanced, with bows and arrows at the ready, up the burnt-out street. The women wore grass skirts, the men had painted faces and the children were smeared with red mud. The intention had been to share some specially slaughtered roast pig and sweet potatoes with the Ambassador as a welcoming gesture but he wasn't waiting around and made a quick exit through the crowd to his waiting car.

His departure (although it left everybody slightly confused) didn't dampen proceedings as leaders got out the megaphone and addressed the crowd. "This visit shows that we need full independence … We need independence this year, not next year, we don't want to accept autonomy, we want full independence. Take pictures and tell the UN we need our human rights," said Alpius Murib, the first speaker, who then ordered everyone to pray before the food was distributed. "We pray that as our people are suffering our friends from overseas come here," he said, "to hear what has

happened here and to share our food and we pray for full independence."
He clasped his hands and bowed his head and so did the crowd. The
speeches went on in the hot sun as the chunks of steaming roast pig were
handed out on leaves. Eli Wantik, a student from West Papua's largest university, Cenderawasih, grabbed the megaphone and delivered the speech
he had wanted to read to the Ambassador in English: "The most important
thing I demand of the United States Ambassador is that he look at the
whole Papuan people and how they were integrated into the state of
Indonesia. The United States people must take responsibility for their
involvement in the scandalous Act of Free Choice and the lack of self-
determination they supported." The crowd clapped enthusiastically as the
speech was translated back to them. Everybody there, despite their tribal
dress and primitive appearance, knew quite well the role the US had
played in supporting first the 1962 New York Agreement that transferred
power from the Dutch to the Indonesians and then the 1969 Act of Free
Choice that ratified it. It was the first time anybody could remember a US
official visiting and they were determined to make their point.

The next morning, outside the main administration building of
Cenderawasih in Abepura, a group of a few hundred protesters waited with
banners for the US Ambassador, simple banners saying "Referendum yes,
autonomy no" or "Referendum – solution for problem of West Papua".
One man just held up a piece of paper with a line drawing of a TNI soldier kicking down a door and threatening a woman with a child in her
arms and beneath it a man with a balaclava and a gun dragging away a
naked woman. Inside the conference hall the Rector of the university was
busy explaining to the Ambassador and the assembled officials, with the
aid of an overhead projector, the benefits of the autonomy package. He
ran through the aims of the package in point form: law enforcement;
clean and good governance; human rights violation investigations;
addressing historical grievances. The Rector and the officials had a hand
in drafting the legislation and supported its implementation, which
brought the university substantially more funding. The Ambassador was

fulfilling the stated aim of the visit – to review the autonomy package. Everybody listened politely and made the occasional note. The student representatives in their blue and yellow jackets whispered to each other in the back rows, passing around a leaflet they hoped to give the Ambassador consisting mainly of photos of Indonesian soldiers standing over dead Papuans. Outside the protestors started chanting *"Papua Merdeka"* ("Freedom for Papua") which could be clearly heard as the Rector's dry speech continued.

Finally it was time for questions and a large Papuan girl, the students' representative, stood up and began to speak. "West Papua doesn't want autonomy," she said. "The Indonesians brought it in, in a clandestine way. I have to talk to you about the problem in my life here. How do I know there will not be reprisals if I speak to you? You can see that the government of Indonesia is not open about our problems. Do you want to put human rights in our society? Do you want to say to the West Papuan people you have to live with that?"

The Ambassador thanked her for her "frank candour" and proceeded to defend his position. He quoted the American Secretary of State, Colin Powell, "We don't go anywhere we are not wanted," as justification for his being there. He said the Papuan problems were raised at the highest levels by his government with the Indonesians. He talked about how the United States believed that "human rights and basic freedoms are universal" and that this was his message to the Indonesians. After the next round of questions from another student, he began to change tack: "I agree that the Papuan people are simply demanding that which has been taken away from them." When asked why the international community seemed to hate the West Papuan people and to express its antagonism by conspiring in their continued isolation, he replied, "I am not sure the people from outside hate the Papuan people as much as they love Papuan resources. I'm not sure which is which," and he chuckled to himself. Another student asked why, now that the Cold War was over (which was Kennedy's rationale for pressuring the Dutch to leave, in order to keep Indonesia out of the Soviet camp), the US could not change its position on West Papua. "It was much simpler for us then," he began. "Today it is much more complicated with human rights, democracy, women's rights, other social trans-national issues are very much a part of what makes Americans what they are and therefore are reflected in our foreign policy." He didn't answer the question and went on to talk about September 11 and that now with the focus on terrorism, the US paid more attention than ever to what happened in West Papua. He talked about finding balances and values and when it was appropriate to stand up for moral principles and when it was not.

The students were getting no clear answers and were losing patience. Finally one asked if America supported the Papuan people or not. The Ambassador replied: "If you leave this room and you say that the US does not support the Papuan people, that's not true. Because that would give the impression that the United States does not care what happens to the Papuan people and that the United States is not prepared to reproach the government of Indonesia ... I hope you don't go out and tell your colleagues that the United States does not support the aspirations of the Papuan people because in a very narrow definition of what that means – independence or not – that would be too simplistic." The Ambassador took this up in his closing remarks, "I support your right to go outside and say whatever you want, so that is really what this is all about." But that wasn't really what it was about. The students understood all too well that his visit had been in support of the autonomy package and that the United States would not back them.

The meeting broke up and the Ambassador and the officials quickly went into a huddle. The chanting outside had grown louder, and the protesters were now on the steps of the building. The student representatives went downstairs and started to address the crowd of people who were chanting that they wanted to see the Ambassador. As the large girl read out into a megaphone what the Ambassador had said, the mood seemed to change. The bloodcurdling Dani war whoops started up again and a group of young men charged up the steps and began pushing the other demonstrators out of the way. People began to run, some to get away, some to join in, some to try and block the group who were trying to force their way into the building. More yellow and blue jacketed students came from inside the building and the doorway was suddenly full of pushing, punching, kicking men who screamed at the people to get back and were answered in turn by the Dani war whoops. The students who moments before had been trying to shame the US Ambassador into admitting the two-faced nature of US policy towards West Papua were now busy trying to keep their pro-independence colleagues from charging through the doors and trashing the building. Car horns at the back of the crowd alerted the struggling mass that the Ambassador and the officials had left the building by a side door and were driving off in their four-wheel drives. The trouble subsided and people stopped pushing, they let go of one another and straightened themselves up. A few gave the doors a desultory parting kick before they walked off.

The violence had flared so suddenly and viciously and then just as quickly abated that everybody was a bit out of breath. "It was another group, not from here, they want to cause trouble for us," said one of the students who had been in the meeting. A post-mortem discussion started outside as the crowd dispersed. Some people said the charging young men had been paid to disrupt the meeting, some said they should have let them in, still others defended their actions by saying the Ambassador should have spoken to the crowd, they had been waiting all morning. It was the West Papua struggle in microcosm. Some believed that they had to follow the rules of civilised dialogue and others thought they had to act now, with as much force as they could muster. Everybody was suspicious, looking for infiltrators, everybody was second-guessing everybody else's motives. The Indonesian attempt to divide and infiltrate the independence movement looked as if it had worked, at least to an extent. And behind all this there was an overwhelming desire for change, for something to happen, for progress – the only question was how. But being met once more with indifference and patronising double-talk from the international community, it was not hard to see why the group of highlanders just wanted to smash the place up in frustration.

Later I asked Ralph Boyce what the US position was. He said the US supported the special autonomy program and thought it was the only way ahead for West Papua. "It is a major historical opportunity for Indonesia to put the past behind it and make good the promise of special autonomy. It is also an opportunity for the people of Papua to put the past behind them because they have had a rough past to be sure and they can work to see the possibilities inherent in special autonomy." He emphasised that US policy supported the territorial integrity of Indonesia and said, "Obviously there are some elements here that you know will accept nothing less than full support for *Papua Merdeka* [Freedom for Papua] but that's just not realistic. That's not really something we are here to look at."

I asked what the US position would be if the independence movement threatened US interests in West Papua, such as the enormous Freeport McMoRan gold and copper mine. "We would take any threats to US interests, including economic interests, seriously. As we have in the past with Exxon Mobil in Aceh. There are ways to express your political grievances and then there are ways that are unacceptable and attacking an economic target, potentially risking innocent lives, is questionable at best," he said.

Free Aceh (GAM) rebel activity closed down the Exxon Mobil Arun gas facility in Aceh, at the other end of Indonesia, for four months in early 2001. An extra 2,128 Indonesian troops were deployed in the area and an operation was conducted to secure the area under Presidential Decree Number 4 issued by President Wahid authorising the army to resume operations in Aceh. The shutdown risked losses to the Indonesian government of US$100 million dollars a month, and four days after the closure the Indonesian cabinet adopted a decision to declare GAM a "separatist" organisation and set in motion preparations for an all-out offensive in Aceh. The offensive started on 2 May 2001 and is still going. 1,700 people died in Aceh in 2001 and more than 500 have died so far in 2002, mostly civilians at the hands of the Indonesian military as it conducts operations to wipe out the independence movement. Exxon Mobil reportedly provides up to 5 billion rupiah (US$560,000) per year to the Indonesian military for protection against Free Aceh. Last August the company was taken to court in the US by the Washington-based International Labour Rights Fund on behalf of eleven Acehnese who had suffered torture at the hands of TNI soldiers who were contracted to "protect" the plant. The lawsuit charged that the Acehnese "have been subjected to serious human rights abuses including genocide, murder, torture, crimes against humanity, sexual violence". Most of these crimes took place in buildings built by Exxon or on land used by it. The plant is now operating again. The relations between the Indonesian military and the Freeport mine are the same. It provides money and facilities to the Indonesian military for protection against the OPM. What Boyce was saying was that if the facility was threatened, the result would be the same. A large and violent military operation would be unleashed to secure the area, bankrolled to some extent by a US company.

The Freeport-McMoRan gold and copper mine in Tembagapura, West Papua is Indonesia's largest single taxpayer and the world's largest gold and third largest copper producer. In 2000 it listed revenue at US$1,868,610,000 – almost 1.9 billion dollars. The history of the Freeport corporation is a rags to riches story of how a small US mining firm won one of the most lucrative mining concessions in one of the most difficult, dangerous and remote areas of the planet. And, in what has been called a miracle of modern engineering, it has turned Freeport into one of the most profitable mining operations in the world. It sounds too good to be true and it is. Much of the mine's success lies in the fact that it has the full repressive power of the Indonesian state working for it against the wishes and the interests of the local inhabitants.

Two years before the Act of Free Choice formally established Indonesian sovereignty over West Papua, Freeport signed its first contract with the Suharto regime. The agreement, the first foreign investment contract signed by Suharto's government, gave Freeport the right to take land and re-settle indigenous people. There was no provision for loss of food gardens, hunting grounds, fishing areas and drinking water. It also gave Freeport the right to "take and use" water, timber and soil from the area. Naturally the local Amungme and Komoro people opposed the mine that destroyed their environment and moved them from their land without compensation or even consultation about what was happening. Human rights violations followed shortly after. The first recorded Indonesian military killings in the area were in 1972 and they have continued to the present day. They started slowly, with forced relocations and the associated problems of starvation and illness in the local population who were moved down to the malarial coast from the mountains where the mine operation is based. When the Freeport slurry pipeline was sabotaged by the OPM in 1977, forcing a halt in production, the military presence increased and full-scale attacks on local communities began.

Freeport paid for a large part of this military activity. Internal documents quoted in a report released in July 2002 by the US-based Robert Kennedy Memorial Center for Human Rights say the company paid for "guard houses and guard posts, barracks, parade grounds and ammunition storage facilities" as well as for offices for two army advisors – a total of US$5,160,770 for the army and US$4,060,000 for the police. The report also cites a one-off cash payment of US$35 million given to the army in 1996 that was to be supplemented by an annual donation of US$11 million annually. The report quotes a former Freeport pilot, Terry Doyle, saying that in the late seventies and early eighties it was common for management to order Freeport helicopter pilots to transport Indonesian military troops on operations against the local population. It lists the previously known incidents of torture and killings and of incarceration in Freeport shipping containers that occurred in 1994 and 1995 and were detailed in a report by the Catholic Church.

The Robert Kennedy Center report was intended to be an assessment of human rights violations from 1967 until the present day in the region around Freeport. It was supposed to be done on the ground, in conjunction with the Jakarta-based legal aid foundation YLBH and ELS-HAM in Jayapura, but Freeport objected and refused to co-operate and then the Indonesian police expelled two of the members of the investigating team from West Papua. At the time of the next attempt to send a team, in September 2000, the situation on the ground in West Papua was deemed too dangerous for the investigators to go ahead. Like the rest of West Papua since Indonesian rule, no human rights investigators have ever been given access to the area near the Freeport mine. Consequently reliable information from these remote areas does not exist and it is easy for both the Indonesians and the managers of Freeport to discredit what word-of-mouth reports do come out.

Goliar Tabuni is the local OPM hero. He is the person who led the sabotage of the Freeport slurry pipe back in 1977 and he claims that his OPM fighters have killed 738 Indonesian soldiers in the area since then. I meet him in one of the small timber houses built by Freeport for the Amungme people several years ago. They are on the outskirts of Timika, the south coast mining town that has turned into an Indonesian boom town from the cash spin-offs of the Tembagapura mine, ninety kilometres to the north. He was involved in the 1996 kidnapping of twelve foreigners in the central highland region to the north of Timika and says the fighting in this area has never really stopped since. He says he witnessed the destruction of an Indonesian helicopter last year when it was used in an operation to drop supplies to Indonesian troops in the field.

"From 2001 I was going to war in the Kali Kopi area near Timika," Tabuni says. "The Indonesian *Kopassus* they say to the people they look for sandalwood but they are really going to look for the OPM. The last helicopter was coming to bring food for the *Kopassus* when it came down. Mr Titus Murib (another commander), he has two bombs he brought from PNG. He throws them into the helicopter. Then *Kopassus* call the army here and then the *Kopassus* go to the place and the OPM are all around – they have one weapon and grenades and bow and arrow – and the soldiers who went up there didn't come back. Thirty-eight Indonesian army died in Kali Kopi." After that the area was bombed every day for over a week but the OPM had run away and none of their people was killed.

Tabuni tells another story about how the Indonesian army uses West Papuans to try and find the leaders still in the jungle. Two Papuans from the Indonesian army base in Timika were given pistols and 10 million rupiah (approximately A$2,000) to go and kill Kelly Kwalik (another well-known leader). "They go out and they kill someone and cut off his hands. They take the hands to the Indonesian commander and he gives them 52 million rupiah each." That apparently happened in February 2002 and, according to Tabuni, the Papuans are still in hiding on Biak Island, with the money. "Now the Indonesian army tries to sell us weapons to trap us. Many times they send messages to me to meet the army commander in Timika but I never come," he says. He is aware of the murder last year of another OPM commander, Willem Onde, who did accept the overtures of the Indonesian military.

Goliar Tabuni re-enacts the way they fired explosive-tipped arrows at the pipeline in 1977. Since then his greatest enemy, he says, has been the Freeport head of security, American Vietnam veteran Tom Green. Tabuni describes him as a leader of *Kopassus* and says that during the fighting in the late seventies and early eighties he was involved in dropping bombs from Freeport-owned helicopters onto the camps of the OPM. He says 1,800 people have died as a direct result of attacks from troops based at the mine. "I want to break down the Freeport mine ... when I break it down, then the UN would come to help," declares Tabuni, thumping the table. But he admits that the security exclusion zone that has now been implemented around the mine site and the slurry line has made any more attacks difficult. He claims as many as 8,000 Indonesian troops and police are deployed currently in the Timika and Tembagapura area and he says he has no weapons any more. Minutes later he pulls a hand-gun out of his bag and laughingly invites me to go and kill some Indonesians with him.

There is a certain amount of rollicking bravado about Tabuni but he becomes serious when he tells me about the time the Indonesians sent foreign "journalists" to kill him. It was in a village called Geselema during the "hostage time" in 1996 when the OPM, led by Kelly Kwalik, took seven foreigners and four Indonesian researchers hostage. After the hostages had gone, TNI and *Kopassus* helicopters broadcast to the people in the jungle urging them to gather, saying that foreign journalists wanted to come and bring food and talk with them. An International Committee of the Red Cross (ICRC) helicopter then arrived, but instead of "journalists" the people were confronted with eight "English" soldiers who leapt out of the helicopter and started firing and throwing grenades. One of the West Papuan leaders, Titus Murib, was shot in the thigh. Tabuni says three of the soldiers in the helicopter were shot but not the pilot and they got away. Six OPM soldiers were killed in the confrontation. After that, he says, "They start war and kill all around the kidnapping place." He tells how the local people ran to the jungle and soldiers were dropped by helicopter on all sides. In one village, he says, "The Indonesian military wanted food so the local people brought them food. They then take the wives of the local people and make local people make a special house and the Indonesian army use them there." He has another story about how villagers gathered in the Mapnduma church house and then the Indonesians dropped a bomb there, killing two children. He then fled with his men to the south near Timika where he is still at large today. The Indonesian offensive, he says, went on for the rest of 1996 in the Mapnduma area.

Tabuni's story tallied with what the Australian reporter Mark Davis found out when he visited Kelly Kwalik in 1997. Davis reported that the ICRC had allowed their helicopter to be used in a military operation with the aim of assassinating the OPM leaders responsible for the kidnapping.

But the Indonesians' stroke of brilliance was to label the white mercenaries (possibly Sandline operatives or British SAS who were working with *Kopassus* to free the hostages) as journalists. The people in the central mountains (particularly the OPM) had only ever seen one journalist venture up there, the Australian Ben Bohane in 1995. After the helicopter attack, they would be suspicious of and hostile to any white person purporting to be a journalist.

And that was largely what happened when two Dutch journalists wandered into the area in 2001. According to the OPM they walked for two weeks from Timika to get to Kiyawagi in the Puncak Jaya range in the centre of the island. They apparently told the villagers that they were important men in the eyes of the Indonesians. "The local commander Titus Murib tell his soldier to kill them but a pastor said don't kill them just send them back." He said the journalists even offered to have themselves kidnapped for a month if they could speak to the leader. But the commander, Titus Murib, who had been wounded in the Mapnduma helicopter skirmish, told them to forget it. The OPM blame the Dutchmen for talking to the Indonesians on their return to Jakarta and for a subsequent military operation. "In Ilaga there is still military operation now. The local people make camps in the bush and not come to the villages. The Indonesians they not kill them just burn down their houses and kill their pigs. The people won't come and stay in the villages. We know about human rights but they [the Indonesians] never change. I don't know exactly how many people die looking for the food," Tabuni says, before explaining that for the highland people, who live mainly on sweet potatoes and pigs, the destruction of their gardens and livestock creates grave food shortages.

When the meeting is finished it is almost midnight and I am driven back to town. We can't go by the most direct route, the sealed highway that runs from Timika to Tembagapura, because access to this road is controlled by the Indonesian military working for Freeport and they have checkpoints at all the crossroads. Instead we drive through the muddy pot-holed roads of the Papuan neighbourhood. The only signs of life are groups of young men armed with spears and bows and arrows. The driver says they are protecting their territory from Laskar Jihad, the Muslim militant group. They're worried the gangs of Indonesian migrants in Timika are going to start something and so young Papuans guard the area all night, every night.

In the morning the driver and a translator come to get me. They are very nervous and say we have to leave this hotel straightaway because there have been some problems. I go to pay the bill and see what he means. There are about thirty men in Muslim skullcaps, some wearing the long white shirt favoured by the Laskar Jihad, waiting at reception. They all stop talking when I come in and just stare. I pay the bill as they gather around. The clerk won't even look at me and demands I fill out the check-in forms again as he has to hand them in to the police. Then he wants to look at my passport and visa again and I say they are in my other bag and I'll be back in a second. The men are already inspecting my papers as I leave. In the car my other companions are laughing. It turns out the hotel I chose was owned by a man from Java who is connected to the Laskar Jihad and when I arrived back late the night before in the company of some Papuans he got suspicious. The men were there to intimidate me or interrogate anybody who came to see me. As we drive out they spill out on to the verandah and glare at our departing car. It is funny but not for my driver and translator who have to live there in Timika.

On a Saturday afternoon in Timika, the town's central market is by turns hot and dusty or wet and muddy. Rotting food lies everywhere and the simple tin shelters that hold the produce are crowded together and crammed with people, mostly young male Indonesians, who come to Timika in their thousands to try to make money. Hundreds of motorcycles roar continually around the dusty roads. It's weird because there is almost nowhere to go. No roads lead anywhere from Timika except up to the mine site in Tembagapura, and access to that is restricted.

As well as the Indonesians, Timika also attracts Papuans who literally walk down from their tribal lands looking for money and employment (in much the same way that the PNG capital Port Moresby attracts those on the other side of the border). Freeport has made a point of employing a small percentage of Papuans in recent years in an attempt to clean up its image. They are mostly employed in the most difficult and dangerous jobs underground, with little hope of advancement.

In the middle of the crowd a fight starts. A well-built Papuan man in cast-off bright orange Freeport overalls is yelling at an Indonesian. The Papuan man is drunk and sweating and his friends, who are also drunk, are trying to pull him away. He towers over the Indonesian but turns to go and then whacks a passing Indonesian on a motorbike, knocking him clear off the bike. There are screams and pushes and shouts and the Papuan man dares his Indonesian victim to have a go, but he gets back on his bike and wisely gets out of there. As the day wears on drunks, mostly Papuan men, are everywhere.

"I can't believe they are drinking when we are dying in the forest," says my translator, who spent time with Mathias Wenda on the border. Ironically, many West Papuans take the same dim view of drinking as the fundamentalist Muslims who form the Laskar Jihad and who began anti-alcohol campaigns when they started arriving in Timika in 2001.

Most of West Papua is still dry due to the influence of the missionaries and the Indonesian authorities who continued the policy. Not in Timika, though. The wild west atmosphere of the town, where people come from all parts of Indonesia to make a quick buck, gets more intense as night falls. Fights break out in the places selling alcohol, and in the alleys and lanes between the shoddily made buildings of corrugated iron and plasterboard. In these alleys the prostitutes, who have descended on the place from all parts of Indonesia, come out for the night. Not surprisingly, HIV is developing into a huge problem in Timika and consequently in the rest of West Papua. The transient nature of the immigrant workforce has heightened the problem along with poor education and poverty among the

Papuans. A recent report by Reverend Barr, an Australian Uniting Church minister who works in West Papua dealing with the current situation, noted:

> I heard a number of stories concerning the increasing incidence of HIV/AIDS in Papua. While I could not obtain precise statistics, the increase in HIV/AIDS is said to be alarming. Many people believe the military have a vested interest here in introducing and perpetuating the problem. The introduction of HIV/AIDS is being undertaken as an effective way of wiping out indigenous people. Alarming rates of HIV/AIDS among remote tribes in the Merauke region is a case in point. This has resulted from the introduction of prostitution in the area and the deliberate offering of favours to local tribal leaders in response to the acquisition of indigenous land for commercial development. Many believe this is a blatant case of ethnic cleansing.

Whether it is simply the result of lack of education concerning HIV or, as Reverend Barr suggests, the result of a plan by the army to spread HIV by providing infected prostitutes, West Papua has the highest rate of HIV in Indonesia (13.3 cases of HIV per 100,000 as compared to 0.325 cases per 100,000 in Indonesia as a whole). Another possible explanation (other than deliberate introduction by the military) is the proximity of West Papua to PNG where, according to an AusAID report released in May 2002, 15,000 people are infected with HIV out of a population of 4.6 million, an infection rate that the report says could wipe out 40 per cent of the adult population in the next twenty years.

In West Papua, where Papuan women have been sterilised against their will in Indonesian hospitals – an abuse which was also widely reported in East Timor – fear of Indonesian medical services exacerbates the problem. Stories of poisonings of leaders, such as the Wamena tribal leader Yafeth Yelemaken in June 2002, also lead Papuans to avoid Indonesian medical authorities at all costs. In an environment where killings by the Indonesian security forces are commonplace and where Papuan leaders have been routinely assassinated by the Indonesian military for the last forty years, it is hardly surprising that people would accuse the military of intentionally spreading HIV. Prostitution (along with logging, fishing and trade in rare birds) is a standard way the TNI in West Papua supplements its operational budget.

Crime is more of a problem in Timika than elsewhere in West Papua and the alcohol fuels this. The presence of the mine and the chance of wealth has created a sprawling dirty city of roughly built shacks on a river polluted with the tailings from the mine, which environmentalists say is an ecological disaster that dwarfs the scale of the Ok Tedi pollution across the border in PNG. Indonesians and Papuans have come here to make their money and the place has a half-built, impermanent air about it, which is not improved by the sight of the original inhabitants staggering around drunkenly in the middle of town. The foreigners are only ever glimpsed going past in buses that are fitted onto the back of semi-trailers as they are transported to and from the mine site.

At the Timika international airport, where you can get a direct flight to Darwin almost every day, there is a yellow 707 permanently parked on the airstrip. Local legend has it that it used to be Elvis Presley's private jet. It is on permanent standby to evacuate the 300 or so foreign workers who work at the mine, just in case things get out of control.

BLOOD SPRAYED THE WALLS

After the US Ambassador's speech at the university, a group of the students wanted me to speak to people who had been beaten in reprisal for an OPM attack on the police station in Abepura in December 2000 (the same one that Mathias Wenda had mentioned). Abepura is about ten kilometres from Jayapura and the home of the province's largest university. The attack had proved the Indonesian military was still prepared to undertake massive reprisals, even on the province's most informed and educated elite, regardless of the international consequences.

It was an old story that had been well reported and I wasn't particularly interested, but with nothing better to do I met them at dusk in the busy market in the centre of Abepura. They led me up through the hills at the back of town and we quickly left the road and followed various winding paths and then a creek bed through the trees that surrounded so many of the widely spaced simple houses where the Papuans lived, away from the centre of town. By the time we arrived at the dormitory on top of the hill we were drenched in sweat and I started to realise the two students were very nervous. Inside, about eight young highland men were sitting on the floor in the bare rooms of the dormitory. This was where the police had come immediately after the attack on the police station. The students with me started demanding that the others go and fetch those who had been here when the police came. A few of those on the floor *had* been there and when they sat down in front of me to tell me the story of the beating and imprisonment they wouldn't look me in the eye. It was very strange to see these extremely big and well-muscled young men with arms like body-builders sitting there so meekly and jumping every time someone came in the room or there was any movement outside.

The story was very simple. Some OPM people attacked the police station about half a kilometre away at about two in the morning of 7 December 2000. These people knew of only one policeman who was killed during the attack and he was beaten to death with a block of wood.

Another policeman and a security guard also died in the immediate aftermath. The attackers had been OPM people looking for weapons, but they only got one. After the primitive attack they fled and the police sounded the alarm and the army came in. Very soon after this trucks of armed *Brimob* (police mobile brigade soldiers – armed as infantry) started arriving. With no way of catching those responsible the police went straight to the highlanders' dormitory, because the attackers were highlanders and most of them were known to support independence. We stood outside and they showed me how the armed police, joined by some Indonesian troops, came from all directions. Some of them showed me how they got away by running up a gully, others spoke of how they were among the twenty-three that were trapped and then herded into trucks with rifle butts and kicks.

In the next twenty-four hours another five residences around Abepura were raided. Over a hundred people, mostly highlanders, were detained and four students had been shot, one killed and one shot in the head. Three more would die from beatings in detention and one would be permanently paralysed. According to some of those who were detained, whom I managed to speak to in the dormitory, the treatment by the police was brutally basic. "They slashed people with knives, hit them with rifle butts and put people's legs under the table and jumped on the table," one student told me. He had been released a few days later. He looked scared to tell me the details as if by talking to me he could find himself in similar trouble again.

Oswald Iten, a Swiss journalist who had been detained on 2 December for taking photos of an independence rally while he was on a tourist visa, was in the prison those who had been rounded up were taken to. He later wrote of what happened to the highland students who were arrested on 7 December, "What I saw there was unspeakably shocking. About half a dozen policemen were swinging their clubs at bodies lying on the floor and, oddly enough, they did not cry out; at most, only soft groans issued from them. After a few long seconds a guard saw me looking and struck his club against the bars of the cell block door. I quickly went back to my usual spot, from where I could still see the clubs, staffs and split bamboo whips at their work. Their ends were smeared with blood and blood sprayed the walls all the way up to the ceiling. Sometimes I saw the policemen hopping up on benches, continuing to strike blows from there or jumping back down onto the bodies below."

Iten writes how at one point a guard came in and told him what was happening was normal when a policeman was killed. Later about three-dozen beaten prisoners were pushed into his already crowded cell. Iten described how one of them died in front of him. "The last one to enter was a large man, who fell over the bodies on the floor and lay there groaning horribly. He tried repeatedly to straighten himself up, only to fall back down again. Now and again the faces of guards appeared at the barred window and looked impassively at the tangle of maltreated bodies. In the back of the big man's head there appeared to be a coin-sized hole through which I believed I could spot some brain tissue. After nearly an hour and a half of groaning and spasmodic movement, his suffering visibly neared its end. About two metres from me, his powerful body raised itself again and his head struck the wall. A final laboured breath issued from him, then his head dropped down onto the cement floor. At last his agony was over. After a while three lackeys came in and dragged the body out." This student was one of three to die from the beatings.

After twelve days in the police jail in Jayapura, Iten was released and expelled from Indonesia. He wrote up the story of his incarceration once he was out of the country. The two main human rights organisations in Abepura were housed within walking distance of where the attack and round-up took place, and shortly afterwards their leaders were detained and questioned when they issued statements deploring the indiscriminate brutality of the police response. Demanius Wakman, head of YLBH, the legal aid institute, and Johannes Bonai, head of ELS-HAM were both arrested and detained overnight. Johannes said later that, "The police only interrogated me and deprived me of sleep but they were trying to say I was involved in the attack." The students arrested were eventually released after it was obvious they had been detained for no other reason than that they were highlanders. An investigation into the incident was initiated by the Indonesian National Human Rights Commission and was supposed to be one of the first test cases for the new human rights courts in Jakarta. When investigators arrived and interviewed students who had been detained, the police, who were not co-operating with the investigators, rounded up twenty of the students for further interrogations. When the commission of inquiry issued a report in April 2001 saying there was reason to believe gross violations of human rights had occurred and that a tribunal should hear the case, the National Police Chief in Jakarta publicly declared that the commission was prejudiced.

No prosecutions have resulted. The students who haven't fled across the border to join Mathias Wenda still live in Abepura in the dormitories that were attacked. They are terrified the police will come back and it will all start again but they want to keep studying and they have nowhere else to live. They looked relieved when I got up to leave and two of them led me off in a different direction from the way I had come.

MUSLIM CLOAKS, MUSLIM SWORDS

In the centre of Abepura there was a crush to get back on the public bus to Jayapura. In the front seat an Indonesian *Kostrad* soldier sat with his gun across his lap and although it was only 8 p.m. an air of tension pervaded the mostly Indonesian passengers who crammed into the bus. Jayapura, situated on the coast about ten kilometres down the hills from Abepura, is a very Indonesianised city and I was told the Indonesian migrants who live there generally don't go out of their enclaves after dark. They are afraid of Abepura and Sentani which have a higher proportion of Papuans. Back in the crowded centre of Jayapura the streets are lit and full of people. Stalls selling CDs and tapes blare out music and display a range of cheap electrical goods, mobile phones, sunglasses and gaudy posters of pop stars and soccer players. Traders from Sulawesi, Java and Bali cram into the two main streets that run down to the harbour where Indonesian naval and passenger ships are moored. There is barely a Papuan face to be seen among the crowds that loiter every night around the market spilling onto the street, eating the cheap food served from stalls and carts. The crowded laneways and streets that run off up the hillsides that surround the city centre are full of one-room houses made of corrugated iron and plywood. They look just like any slum in Java, which is what they are – Javanese slum dwellings transplanted over the years along with the almost one million Indonesians brought here by Suharto's transmigration scheme.

Local Papuan leaders note how the arrival of Indonesians, sponsored by the army, has picked up in the last year. They talk of thousands of new arrivals coming across on the inter-island *Pelni* ships every week. They say there are at least seven ships a week, each bringing up to 1,000 new arrivals, mostly young men. Their passage is paid for by the army.

When a ship comes in, the dock is crowded with thousands of people pushing to get off and get on. Soldiers line up with their heavy bags and weapons, going home on long-awaited rotations, and immigrants carrying boxes on their heads push their way down the gangplank. It is a huge anonymous mass of angry, shouting, pushing human beings that eventually spews out through the harbour gates into the street crowded with trucks and minibuses and motorbikes. It is at a remove from anywhere else in West Papua. The lines of people at the long distance phone booths, the guy selling *soto Makassar* (spicy entrail soup, a Javanese favourite) from a stall, the beeping army trucks full of troops embarking or arriving, the characters selling sleeping mats and bottled water and packets of noodles for those getting the week-long voyage back to Java. There is a feeling of restless homesickness in the crowds pushing to get on the boat, back to Java and the centre, away from what many of them see as a place to come and make money or a place they have been sent to.

Jayapura is a town that looks to the rest of Indonesia for its survival, whether in the form of government money or goods brought in by sea to trade. The rugged mountains that surround it and make it seem crowded in fact seal it off from the rest of West Papua and constitute what is a psychological screen for the Indonesians who live and work there, making money and administering a territory most of them never see. It's a colony, and the Indonesians have tried to recreate the feeling of an Indonesian city, one they can feel comfortable in and work in. You get the feeling they are only at ease in the crowded streets and alleys of the town centre and not the mountains beyond, which are full of people they nervously deride as savages and whom they laugh at for their lack of sophistication but whom in reality they fear.

According to the latest Indonesian government census conducted in 2000, only 65 per cent of West Papua's population of 2,233,530 people are now of indigenous descent. The rest have come to West Papua chiefly through the massive transmigration program run by former Indonesian president Suharto during the seventies and eighties in which mostly poor landless farmers were relocated by the Indonesian government to West Papua. Transmigration only ceased in the late nineties and there began an exodus of roughly 60,000 Indonesians from the province as the urban-based pro-independence movement led by the Presidium made its presence felt. The loss of East Timor in September 1999 further impressed upon Indonesian settlers that there was no future in a soon to be independent – or, in any case, disputed – West Papua, and the numbers leaving increased to a flood.

Just recently, the tide has turned again as the Indonesian military seeks to exploit the current ethnic mix by sponsoring the Muslim militants Laskar Jihad (recently embroiled in the sectarian fighting in the Moluccas, the next island chain to the west of Papua) and supporting militia groups to create conflict between the communities – conflict that will inevitably end in the military intervening on the side of their countrymen, the settlers.

"Papuans don't want it but they are using Indonesians who have been in Papua a long time and also with the transmigrants so we don't know whether they will succeed or not with this latest plan," says Presidium leader Thom Beanal. "It is difficult for us. We don't have the power to say it is not allowed for a lot of ships to come in. Yesterday we took the decision to refuse these ships coming in and we also want to reject the army presence here but we don't know if it will work or not."

Dr Greg Poulgrain, a lecturer in South East Asian Studies and frequent visitor to West Papua, revealed the existence of a high-level document from Jakarta in the *Courier Mail*. The document, from February 2002, outlined increased transmigration as being one of three ways to counter Papuan nationalism (the other two being political assassinations and increased intelligence operations). According to Poulgrain, the aim of the transmigration is to destabilise the current 60–40 ratio in favour of Papuans over non-Papuans in the province. He also pointed out that the overwhelming number of young men among the new arrivals provides a recruiting pool for militia and Laskar Jihad activity.

Beanal echoes Poulgrain, saying there is a program that sponsors the arrival of Muslim militants from the Laskar Jihad group to stir up problems between the mainly Christian Papuans and the Muslim settlers from other parts of Indonesia. He says there has also been a program funded by the army to recruit East Timor-style militias to fight pro-independence Papuans. The two groups – Muslim militants and militias – share the same aims and backers: "The Laskar Jihad, I've heard they are Muslims but from the army. They want to have a religious conflict in Fak Fak [an eastern town in West Papua] but we don't respond, so they say they are from the Red and White militia, then provoke us. Papuans don't want it but they are using Indonesians who have been in Papua a long time and also transmigrants so there will be fighting between us."

In the ramshackle transmigrant settlement of SP3 on the outskirts of Sorong, at the far western tip of West Papua, the Papuans no longer venture out after dark. Every night towards midnight armed groups of men wearing black headbands set up posts blocking the roads to certain areas and other figures begin arriving by truck and motorbike. These are the zealots of Laskar Jihad and they use the hours between 11 p.m. and 3 a.m., when the power is out in the village, to conduct training sessions with guns, bombs and swords to prepare for what locals in Sorong fear will be a reprise of the religious violence in Ambon.

Local residents say that outside SP3 these activities have been happening for over a year and they are terrified by the blatant involvement of members of the police and the military. Residents report the regular appearances of nine armed and uniformed *Brimob* (police mobile brigade) members at the nightly training sessions and the introduction of nocturnal TNI and *Kopassus* patrols in an area when they were previously unknown. "Seven Pakistanis came here and spoke in all the mosques around here. We hear what they are doing and we see the training every night and we are very worried. We feel that if there is an incident here the situation will explode," said a Papuan resident who refused to be identified. Non-Muslim residents are forbidden to enter the perimeter of the training camps and several have been beaten up for disobeying. In early May a Papuan man was knocked down by a carload of Laskar Jihad members who then threatened him with knives, according to this witness.

He then related the story of how his son had been with a small Muslim child, one of the newcomers, who was playing with a steel cable and who said his father would use the cable to kill all the Papuans.

Sorong has a population of 114,000. The mix is roughly 50 per cent Papuan and 50 per cent migrants from Indonesia. The transmigration camps were first set up here in the late seventies and the logging and local oil production has made it a relatively stable and prosperous place. It is free of the regular outbreaks of military violence that have accompanied calls for independence and OPM activity in the Wamena, Jayapura, Timika and Biak areas.

But local workers from ELS-HAM, the human rights monitoring group, paint a different picture; they speak of the appearance of weapons in their community and the manufacturing of bombs and the secretive arrival and subsequent training of up to 3,000 members of Laskar Jihad. They talk of an increasing tension in the province between Muslim settlers and Christian Papuans that is being contrived by the military in collusion with the Laskar Jihad, who have been arriving from nearby Ambon in increasing numbers throughout 2002. The conflict in Ambon has been going since 1998 with estimates of between 5,000 and 10,000 people killed. Laskar Jihad sent 2,000 "warriors" to Ambon in 2000. The move is credited with re-igniting the conflict because the Laskar Jihad members are said to have worked hand in hand with the Indonesian military who were partisan on the side of the Ambonese Muslims. On 4 May 2002, twelve Christian villagers were killed in a raid carried out by Indonesian soldiers and Laskar Jihad fighters despite a recent ceasefire which had come into effect on 30 April. Laskar Jihad leader, Jaffar Umar Thalib, has publicly declared his intention to fight the "separatists" in West Papua.

In Sorong they recruit and train members from among the new Muslim settlers and the 9,000 Ambonese refugees already there. Sorong is about to be made an example of to the rest of West Papua, ELS-HAM says, with communal violence fostered by the military in order to reassert the military's control.

In March 2000, *Satgas Papua* (the pro-independence West Papuan militia) raided a house and found seven M-16s. The two men who lived there, Serka Samper, an intelligence officer with the local Indonesian military command, and a police officer by the name of Putrilio, had been seen organising the first Laskar Jihad training sessions. The weapons were handed in to the police but the two men were never charged. This was the first incident involving weapons in Sorong and they have continued ever since, according to ELS-HAM. "There was a small boat in June last year that arrived here full of weapons, the police impounded it but we don't know what happened and no one was ever charged. Seven boxes of weapons and ammunition were seen being unloaded from a truck by Laskar Jihad members early this year and in January we see Laskar Jihad members carrying pistols right here in the centre of Sorong." Louis Kaitana from ELS-HAM says the Laskar Jihad members also bring their own weapons, including homemade muskets, parangs and bombs.

ELS-HAM has identified twelve places in the Sorong region where training camps have been established. The nearest are in the transmigration camps that start on the outskirts of town and the furthest is in the south coast village of Segon, where there is only access by boat. "We are very worried about the camp in Segon because local people tell us many boats have been coming and going but there are no police or army in the area and there is very little communication with the local people down there so we don't know what they are doing there," says Louis. Deliberate provocations by Laskar Jihad are already underway, says Paskalis Baru, the director of ELS-HAM in Sorong: "There was a young woman student who studied in SP3. The Laskar Jihad gave her a bomb to bomb the church and they pay her money. The local people found the bomb and destroyed it. That was in April." Paskalis claims the body of a dead Christian Ambonese man was dumped outside the local Catholic Church this Easter. The police removed the body but there has been no further report.

The involvement of the police and military in the establishment of Laskar Jihad in Sorong is an open secret. The local police commander,

Faisal Abdul Nasser, was a founding member in 2001 of the Sorong branch of Surnah Wal-Jamaah, an Indonesia-wide Islamic organisation that supports Laskar Jihad. The local military commander is also a member.

A colleague and I went to visit the small plain office of the organisation that serves as a front for Laskar Jihad in Sorong. The office was full of Arabic texts and we sat on a rug on the floor. A man with a wispy beard explained that, yes, they had come from Ambon and Java and they were just here to proselytise the Muslim faith "like missionaries".

He told us there were only seven of them there. My colleague began to question him. What about Ambon? "There was external interference in the Maluku problem from Holland – these people from outside who are deliberately trying to break up Indonesia, the Dutch NGOs who see Indonesia as an occupier." He went on to explain that when it is peaceful they are peaceful people but of course if there are problems they must fight. My colleague, who had recently been in Aceh and Ambon, asked how the Laskar Jihad could support an army crackdown on Acehnese Muslims, who are known to be good Muslims, by an army (TNI) made up of both Muslim and Christian soldiers. The man responded that the interests of one group of Muslims (in Aceh) could not be equated with the interests of the (global) Muslim community as a whole. He then added that some Muslims weren't as good as others. When asked about the connection between Islam and the unitary republic of Indonesia he replied that because Indonesia is a Muslim country, preserving the unitary state is in the interests of Islam.

The politeness of the meeting disappeared when my colleague began asking about West Papua. "We would support the Muslims if they were attacked here. We would have to bring people here," he said, adding, "The Papuans need to prove they have been marginalised. The question is, 'Are the Papuans capable of managing gold and oil?' If they are they have to prove it." The spokesman's young assistant wrote down his replies in a notebook. In the manner of a teacher or sage, the speaker sat cross-legged on the floor dispensing what to him were obvious truths. He gave his name as Shafruddin and said there were only seven of them here and that their business was to teach and he knew nothing of any training program. We said our goodbyes and left. It was obvious we were getting nowhere but my colleague's line of questioning had revealed the Islam of nationalist bent that was at the heart of their vision and policy. It was an Islam that aggressively supported the state of Indonesia and the actions of the TNI.

In April the US Ambassador, Ralph Boyce, met local leaders from Sorong in Jayapura to discuss the rising tension. The police and military commanders and the local *Bupati* (mayor) all told him not to believe the reports of the NGOs and the church leaders regarding Laskar Jihad activity in the area and insisted there were no problems.

According to the local Protestant minister, Martin Luther Wanma, the local police chief even suggested Laskar Jihad members be used as security forces when a pro-independence demonstration was planned last December. "The people here feel uneasy. They know what Laskar Jihad has done in Maluku and Poso (Sulawesi). They think the Laskar Jihad are like Satan. Laskar Jihad say they come here not to fight but to teach like the missionaries but the people here don't believe them, they remember Poso and the Malukus," he says. This outspoken pastor says he fears the worst if trouble starts because he knows the eye-for-an-eye culture of the Papuans. "It is a strong culture. If you kill my brother … I have to kill you." He says he warned the military commander at a recent meeting, "You be careful. If you do this, my people will kill many Indonesians."

The nervous Papuan residents of SP3 see the conflict in the same way. Recently representatives of the local OPM commander came to see them about the training of Laskar Jihad. "The OPM come here and tell us they are monitoring the Jihad with radios and that if they attempt anything they will make war with them," said one resident. "But we know they are close to the TNI so it would just make things worse … Once the OPM do it, the conflict will explode." And that is exactly what the Indonesian military wants.

In a simple two-roomed wooden shack in the mining town of Timika, Yosefa Alomang tells me her story surrounded by three generations of her family. On 10 November 1999, they raised the Morning Star flag near the Catholic church in Timika. "We were in the car and we were taking pictures of all the people dancing. The Indonesian army came and took Mr Alpius and his mother and they took the camera and all the documents. They shoot one girl. There is a very old lady crying near the flag because they try to pull it down and the soldiers shoot her. Six people, three men and three women, were killed that day. They take all the leaders and bring them to the prison and they release them shortly after." She hands me a card from the Australian embassy in Jakarta. It is from the third secretary, Jo Leong. She says she got it when she met him in January 2000 and passed on to him documents detailing human rights abuses in the Timika area. She says she also spoke to the Dutch embassy.

Raising of the Morning Star flag is the most common form of civilian protest against Indonesian rule. The first post-Suharto flag-raising took place in Biak in July 1998 where eight people were killed guarding the flag and as many as 150 killed in a subsequent massacre. Since then Amnesty International has reported flag raisings in Sorong (July 1999, August 2000), Timika (November 1999), Nabire (February and March 2000), Merauke (February, November and December 2000), Fak Fak (December 2000) and Manokwari (May 2001). Amnesty estimates the number of deaths as a result of military retaliation to be at least thirty-seven but admits the exact figures are unclear because the Amnesty workers were ejected in 2002 before they could finish their work. They also emphasise that dozens of other West Papuans have been shot and injured and imprisoned following these flag raisings. In January 2002 the Amnesty delegation investigating human rights abuses was asked to leave West Papua by the authorities after it was mistakenly reported in the local press that they were conducting an investigation into the death of Theys Eluay.

There is an almost religious quality to the belief that raising the Morning Star flag will somehow assist in the struggle against foreign domination. The history of the Morning Star flag goes back to Dutch colonial times in the late nineteenth century when followers of the nationalistic *Koreri* movement spread the idea of flying the Dutch tricolour flag upside down to invert the moral status of the roles of the Dutch colonisers and the Papuan people. Then the Morning Star was added to signify the star that guided *Manseren*, the god figure of the movement who would one day return and lead the Papuan people to a heavenly existence on earth. Prophets were called *Konor* and frequently led their people in uprisings against the Dutch. When the Japanese arrived in early 1942, the independence fighters resisted them. After an Allied bombing raid on Manokwari in which only Japanese were killed, one leader, Stephanus, declared that this was a testament to the Papuan destiny. He took a series of demands to the Japanese, including the return of West Papua to its original inhabitants and the right to fly the Morning Star flag. The Japanese executed him. Another group of *Koreri* followers were machine-gunned en-masse when they turned out to fight the Japanese in Biak with sticks they believed *Manseren* would turn into rifles.

Once it was clear to the West Papuans that the Indonesians (who had replaced the Dutch) were not going to implement self-determination through the Act of Free Choice, there were many acts of resistance. The most serious uprising produced the fighting near Manokwari in the mid-sixties. Mark Worth, an Australian filmmaker who has worked extensively in West Papua, says the fighting involved more than 9,000 villagers and required the bringing in of 14,000 Indonesian troops to quell it. The rebellion was started by seventy-year-old Johan Ariks who had been educated by Catholics in Java as a result of his father having been taken there as a slave. When he returned and started to preach rebellion against the Indonesians he was treated as a *Konor* or prophet of *Manseren* by the local people, and the local Papuan police left behind by the Dutch took their weapons and followed him. As the referendum on the Act of Free Choice approached, Suharto placed the notorious General Sarwo Edhie (the man who oversaw the mass killings of suspected communist sympathisers that followed Suharto's rise to power in 1965) as overlord of the operation to wipe out the rebellion. The villagers had found a large cache of World War II weapons left by the American forces and they used them to devastating effect against the not much better armed Indonesians. "So you would have had the Indonesians strafing them with ex-US B25 Mitchell bombers and the people fighting back with .50 calibre machine guns," Worth said. "It is amazing a war that big was fought for so long with so little attention."

Johan Ariks eventually was captured in 1967 and died in jail. The two Mandatjan brothers, who were leaders in the Manokwari region, finally surrendered to the Indonesians in January 1969. They had controlled 10,000 villagers and had held out against the Indonesians ever since the Dutch left in 1963 but they had gradually been worn down by relentless aerial bombing, by strafing and the destruction of their villages by ground troops. They were flown to Jakarta and, as a face-saving gesture, Lodewijk Mandatjan was dressed in an Indonesian major's uniform. Arriving in the same plane was Fernando Ortiz Sans, the UN bureaucrat who would oversee the Act of Free Choice. The two Mandatjan brothers were later quietly killed in Java. The only leader left at large from the rebellion was Fritz Awom who defiantly sent a message to the Indonesians saying they would have to catch him and hang him in the Manokwari marketplace before he stopped fighting. It is believed he was killed later in the bush.

Because of the deaths at the flag raising in Timika in 1999, Yosepha says she decided to lead a delegation to Jakarta in January 2000. "The Presidium never reports these things," she says. "Thom Beanal and Theys Eluay cannot report what people are saying. Nothing ever changes." She believes that her local human rights office in Timika is a business project that exists only to secure funding from the government and says the people are rightly suspicious of it. When she was in Jakarta and told the stories of the people from Timika to the Indonesian parliament, she says the leader of the parliament stood up and told her they would get independence. "But we come back and wait and nothing happens," she says. "They keep killing us in many ways ... They want to kill us all."

OPM fighters prepare to raise the Morning Star flag at their border camp.

Raising of the Morning Star flag.

Fighters training at the OPM border camp.

ANOTHER EAST TIMOR

On the afternoon of 19 May 2002, the world's media congregated inside a small, hot converted shipping container next to Dili's newly re-built Comoro airport. CNN noisily prepared to go live to air as journalists wiped sweat from their notepads and conferred quietly among themselves. Finally, UN Secretary-General Kofi Annan arrived in advance of the festivities that would carry on through the night as East Timor celebrated its hard-won freedom. Annan was there to attend the independence ceremony, but even more importantly in most people's eyes, officially to hand over sovereignty of the territory from the United Nations (who had taken it from the Indonesians in October 1999) to the people of East Timor. After praising the East Timorese and saying they had "earned their freedom" and declaring how happy he was that within twelve hours East Timor would finally join the family of nations, Annan answered questions from the hovering reporters. One of the first questions was about the United Nations position on that other part of Indonesia where the UN had been involved, West Papua, and the campaign to have the Act of Free Choice reviewed. "East Timor was not part of Indonesia," the Secretary-General was quick to say. "The UN respects the territorial integrity of Indonesia. We are not going to break up Indonesia and create several East Timors" he said, and tersely called for the next question. With Indonesian President Megawati Sukarnoputri about to arrive to attend the celebrations (against the wishes of the Indonesian military), it was hardly an auspicious moment for a statement on West Papua. But his position could not have been clearer. West Papua was simply not on the agenda.

A few days later East Timor's foreign minister, the Nobel Peace Prize winner Jose Ramos Horta, took the same line. "You will not find one single UN bureaucrat who will stick his neck out in this case. You will not find one single country, with the exception of Nauru, Vanuatu, a few small Melanesian countries … I wouldn't say their case is hopeless because that is what they said about East Timor, although the two situations are slightly different," he said.

Horta said the only way forward for West Papua was to accept the autonomy offered by Jakarta, "because the international community supports autonomy for Aceh and West Papua. So if they play their cards right they are going to have the best international support for the best possible autonomy for them. Then bit by bit they can consolidate their own footholds in the economy, ease out the military power and so on. If they keep on making their demands for a referendum and independence they are not going to get the support of the international community." The East Timorese leadership has since stated publicly that it does not support independence for West Papua. "The fact of the matter is Indonesia cannot afford to lose West Papua," Horta says. "I just don't see a single scenario where the Indonesians will leave." It is easy to see why East Timor's leaders feel they cannot support those still struggling for what they themselves recently attained at such great cost. When the UN and the peacekeepers leave (according to the current schedule in mid-2004), East Timor will still be a country reliant on foreign aid and surrounded by a hostile power, Indonesia.

The current Australian government position on West Papua is straight-forward. No mention is ever made of having another look at the Act of Free Choice or of responding to the demands of the people of West Papua for self-determination, other than to say that Australia hopes the Indonesians will not respond to such wishes with force. In fact, Australia supports Indonesian territorial integrity as it is currently conceived of by the Indonesian government. Prime Minister John Howard made this point clearly during his visit to Jakarta on 6 February this year. The statement from the Australian Department of Foreign Affairs was crystal clear: "Australia wants to see the welfare and the human rights of the people of Papua advanced in the context of a United States of Indonesia. Australia welcomes the implementation of special autonomy for Papua on 1 January this year. Implemented effectively this will improve political and cultural rights of Papuans and return major economic benefits to the province. Australia is urging Indonesia to continue to pursue non-military solutions to separatist demands."

Neither the Australian nor the East Timorese position bears any relation to what is unfolding in West Papua. Within Papuan society the autonomy proposal has not been accepted as a solution, and the Indonesians are responding with military force to Papuan demands. It is clear that the 1999 sacking of East Timor by the Indonesian military in the presence of the United Nations has not led to any change in international policy on West Papua. And the violence in West Papua today is being orchestrated by the same figures in the Indonesian military who were behind the events in East Timor.

The current TNI Commander in West Papua, Major-General Mahidin Simbolon, had the job of providing logistical support to the militia in East Timor in 1999. As chief of staff of the Udayana military district that included East Timor, Simbolon had a long career in covert counter insurgency operations there and had previously worked with *Kopassus* in establishing the SGI military intelligence unit in Dili that was notorious for the routine torture of suspected pro-independence supporters. Six of his assistants were called to testify at the Commission of Inquiry into Human Rights Violations in East Timor (KPP-HAM) hearings.

One of his leading henchmen, now in West Papua, is Lieutenant Colonel Yayat Sudrajat, who also has a background in covert operations in East Timor. He distributed money and weapons to militia in East Timor in 1999 and was also involved in the Liquica massacre in April of that year. When called on to testify at the KPP-HAM hearings in Jakarta in September 2000, he said he was simply doing his job. He has since been assigned to serve under Lieutenant Colonel Hartomo, the commander of the Hamadi *Kopassus* base where Theys Eluay had dinner on the night he was killed. Hartomo also has a history in East Timor. He was mentioned as a possible suspect at a Timor war crimes tribunal and has also been linked to a series of arrests and disappearances in East Timor in 1996. He is the most senior of the ten *Kopassus* members to be charged over the death of Eluay. The facts are plain and they cannot be over-emphasised. The evidence clearly indicates that the whole repressive network of the Indonesian military that laid waste to East Timor is now operating in West Papua.

Australia, and particularly the government of John Howard which gained enormous political mileage from sending in troops to stop the violence in East Timor, has sent a very clear signal to those in charge of the military in Indonesia that things can return to business as usual. The most important element of this message has been the Australian silence at the calculated way in which the truth of what happened in East Timor is being hidden from the Indonesian people in the current farcical trials of those accused of crimes against humanity. The United Nations said the Indonesians were to be given at least the opportunity to try those responsible themselves before any international tribunal would be considered, and so the ad hoc human rights tribunal was set up. After numerous delays and a narrowing of the terms of reference (so that it is only hearing matters relating to a minimal period of two months in 1999), the tribunal got under way in March 2002. None of the senior military commanders was brought to trial and those who were only faced charges of "failing to prevent" the massacres and killings that did take place, not of perpetrating them.

At the time of writing only seven of the verdicts concerning the eighteen East Timorese civilians, police and military commanders had been handed down. East Timor's former governor under the Indonesians, Abilio Osorio Soares, was sentenced to three years in jail on 14 August – well short of the ten years called for by the prosecution. Soares, a notoriously corrupt East Timorese, is the fall guy for the Indonesian military.

Indonesia's last police chief in East Timor was acquitted of all charges along with three colonels and two majors from the police and the army. No observers are under any illusion that justice will be done in the cases of the other eleven charged. The Australian Foreign Minister Alexander

Downer's response was, to say the least, understated, "We have some concerns about what has happened."

The US-based activist John Miller, who has been monitoring the trials, said of them, "The prosecution bought the military myth that the violence in 1999 was the result of conflict between East Timorese factions. Yet the razing of East Timor undeniably resulted from an orchestrated plan by top Indonesian military and other officials to first intimidate the East Timorese into voting to remain under Indonesian rule and then punishing them when they supported independence." It is precisely the same military figures who were notably absent from the lists of the accused at the tribunal who are now running the program in West Papua and the message they are getting from the UN, Australia and the US is that the present tribunal represents an entirely adequate response to the crimes committed.

The US Secretary of State, Colin Powell, visited Jakarta as part of his South-East Asia trip to shore up support for America's war on terror. He announced on 2 August 2002 that the Bush administration planned to spend US$50 million over three years to fund Indonesia's anti-terrorism struggle. And where will this end up? The majority of that money will go to Indonesia's police force, whose human rights record in Aceh and West Papua is as dismal as that of the military's.

The army would receive US$400,000 worth of training under the International Military Education and Training Program (IMET) that had been halted after the human rights abuses in East Timor in 1999. The resumption reflects concerns that Indonesia, as the world's largest Muslim nation, could become a haven for the al-Qaeda network but it is well known inside Indonesia that groups like Laskar Jihad are domestic creations of the Indonesian military. As Sidney Jones, the Indonesia Project Director for the International Crisis Group (the Brussels-based "think tank" currently headed by Gareth Evans), commented to Associated Press on 11 August, "If you scratch any radical Islamic group in Indonesia, you will find some security forces involvement." Analysts say that the American push to re-establish military ties with the Indonesians is part of a long-running strategy to provide a counter-balance to China in South-East Asia. Either way the message is clear. The Bush administration does not consider the token nature of the ad hoc human rights tribunal on East Timor, the continuing repression in West Papua or the outright war being waged by the TNI in Aceh as sufficient reason not to resume its support of Indonesia and its repressive military.

In West Papua itself the deaths continue. On 22 June 2002 Yafet Yelemaken, a tribal chief and a member of the Papuan Presidium Council in Wamena, died from poisoning by the Indonesian military. He was still under house arrest for inciting a riot that had broken out in Wamena on 6 October 2000. The irony was that he had been trying to stop the violence. Since then several other pro-independence figures in Wamena have been followed and interrogated by the military. The story put out by the local police was that these people were under suspicion for trying to create a "Laskar Kristen" or Christian militia to counter the growing number of Laskar Jihad in the area. It is understood that this is being used as a pretext for their arrest.

Benny Wenda, the leader of the *Demmak* highlanders' association, was arrested in Jayapura on 8 June 2002 and is still in police custody where, according to human rights reports, he is being tortured. On 21 August 2002 he was reported to be in bad health, coughing blood, either from beatings or tuberculosis. He was accused of involvement in the December 2000 Abepura attack on the police station and of possessing a PNG passport.

The office of the human rights monitoring group ELS-HAM in Abepura has become increasingly difficult to contact. Calls made from outside the country frequently do not get through and the staff believe the international connection has been cut. They issued a report condemning "Operasi Adil Matoa", a police operation that targets separatist groups. On 17 July 2002 the West Papua police chief, Made Mangku Pastika, issued a letter to all police stations in West Papua ordering them to commence operations targeting the separatists. The ELS-HAM report from 18 July reads,

"This operation named 'Adil Matoa' was the result of the meeting held between President Megawati and provincial governors in Jakarta yesterday in which the President urged the governors to take immediate stern actions against any separatist movement emerging in the provinces, notably Aceh, Papua and Maluku."

ELS-HAM co-ordinator John Rumbiak is one of the main proponents of the Zone of Peace in West Papua. To effect it, ELS-HAM is lobbying the local police to halt the anti-separatist program. ELS-HAM members also meet with the local OPM commanders and seek to dissuade them from responding to provocation by the military and police. On 12 August 2002 Rumbiak travelled to the island of Biak where thirty *Brimob* (police mobile brigade) soldiers had deployed near a remote village to try to arrest the local OPM leader Melkianus Awom. Rumbiak plans to meet with Awom to dissuade him from responding with force. The police have issued warrants for five local OPM leaders and say they will take the offensive in West Biak if the leaders don't hand themselves in. Melkianus Awom was one of the founders of the OPM in Manokwari in 1964 and has been in Biak since 1968. Military operations to wipe out the OPM on Biak killed 600 civilians between 1968 and 1990, and the leader of the movement has been in the jungle for thirty-six years. This decision to target a reclusive leader – whose followers are armed only with traditional weapons – is, according to ELS-HAM, the forerunner of "Operasi Adil Matoa" and a taste of the horrors to come.

On 15 August 2002 Major-General Simbolon was quoted in the local Jayapura paper, the *Cenderawasih Post*, as saying that in Biak the military continued to pursue a "persuasive" approach towards armed separatist groups but given the danger these elements represented to the integrity of Indonesia the army might take "repressive" action and would do so "without compromise".

On the same day in Suva, exiled West Papuan leader Rex Rumakiek told Pacific island press representatives that the same elements who had tried to prevent East Timorese independence were now emerging in West Papua and that unless something was done there would be similar bloodshed in West Papua. A group of West Papuan leaders had traveled to Suva to canvass support among the sixteen-member Pacific Island Forum (including Australia and New Zealand), then meeting in Suva, for a UN review of the 1969 Act of Free Choice.

In Abepura ELS-HAM was concerned that a recent statement by the newly installed TNI chief, General Edriartono Sutarto, said that "efforts to separate from the unitary republic of Indonesia would be crushed with military operations"; they feared this could be part of a program to eliminate the Papuan Presidium Council on the grounds that it was a separatist movement.

Another report from ELS-HAM on 21 July detailed the activities in the border region. A new military battalion from the former Aceh command in Northern Sumatra has arrived in the area between Jayapura and the border and has already established itself in the timber trade by forcing villagers at gunpoint to hand over their processed timber. In two cases villagers were beaten and threatened; on another occasion a man was actually shot at to make him hand over his timber. Another group of villagers was made to eat dirt at gunpoint. Eleven women have been raped in the region in the last two months, reportedly by members of an East Java battalion which has recently moved there.

Mathias Wenda and his men on the border have noticed an increase in Indonesian military activity in the last month with the Indonesian military felling trees in the northern border area. A report in the Port Moresby Post Courier on 9 August 2002 stated that the pressure was about to be increased on the Papua New Guinea side with the PNGDF seeking permission from the National Security Agency Council to move against Wenda and his men and apprehend them. The report quoted one defence force official as saying, "Mr Mathias Wenda seems to be harassing our local people. They are operating on our side of the border."

The previous week the PNG officials had returned from Jayapura where they had held their annual joint border talks. No doubt the Indonesians had raised the matter and the PNGDF felt obliged to act. Or perhaps the commanders in Vanimo felt it was time to start repaying some of the favours they had received from their Indonesian military friends.

Wenda's men are among 11,600 refugees still living in border camps. They are stuck in a limbo with no medical or food support other than that provided by the Catholic Church in Vanimo. Several of them told me stories of going down to Port Moresby over the years and trying to see the Australian High Commission in the hope of being granted asylum in Australia. None of them has ever succeeded. With the Indonesian military trying to provoke the OPM into a fight by moving into border areas where they have traditionally trained, and the PNGDF now co-ordinating with the Indonesians, it seems that the stage is set finally to get rid of them. They have lived off the land for the last thirty years, however, and will probably abandon their makeshift huts and move further into the bush. The fight for independence will continue and the guns will come from somewhere – in all likelihood PNG – where there are plenty of people prepared to swap the OPM's alluvial gold for weapons. The autonomy plan and the military and police programs in West Papua will inevitably provoke more resentment among the Papuans, and if the international community, particularly Australia, continues to ignore the peaceful demands of the Papuan Presidium Council for a genuine act of self-determination, another long and drawn-out cycle of violence is inevitable directly to Australia's north.

As the Chifley government and Dr Evatt recognised at the time of Indonesia's formation in 1949, the West Papuans have always had more in common with their neighbours in Papua New Guinea than they do with the Indonesians. Australia's policy throughout the late forties and most of the fifties was to support the Dutch as long as they worked towards self-determination for the people of Papua, as Australia was doing across the border in PNG. The idea that the two territories should be unified eventually was also supported by both the Australians and the Dutch. But as the Indonesian campaign to acquire West Papua gained momentum in the late fifties and the importance of Indonesia as an ally in the politics of the Cold War dawned on the United States, Australia, under Menzies, was pressured to drop support for the idea of self-determination, which it did in 1959. The intervening forty-three years have not stopped the calls for self-determination in Papua and the worst predictions of Australian policy makers in the 1950s (who argued against the inclusion of West Papua in Indonesia) have largely come true. Perhaps it is time for the Australian government to address the problem once again, before West Papua descends into the kind of mayhem our soldiers so belatedly had to deal with in East Timor.

And perhaps the mayhem is starting. On 31 August, unidentified gunmen shot at Freeport employees on the road to Tembagapura. Two Americans and one Indonesian were killed and twelve others were injured.

The Indonesian military immediately blamed the OPM, and human rights groups blamed the Indonesian military, suggesting money and contract disputes as a motive. The Presidium Council denied any link between the armed groups of the OPM and the attack, calling for Papua to become a Zone of Peace.

News reports suggested that "Goliath [sic] Tabuni and Titus Murib" might be responsible for the attack and referred to them as breakaways from the OPM. On 3 September I received a phone call from a payphone in PNG from a man I had met with Goliar Tabuni. He said they had "big problems" and had just escaped from Timika. Before I could be sure they were responsible for the attack, the phone cut off. Did the attack prefigure their plan to recommence the war in West Papua out of frustration with the Presidium, or was it the work of Papuans in the pay of the Indonesian military, or the military itself? In any case, the reprisals have begun. After forty years of vain struggle and continuous repression and exploitation, it's not hard to see why such a bold action might be contemplated. But nor is it hard to see how it would play into the hands of the Indonesians or how they could entice desperate men to take deadly action.

SOURCES

Essay sources and occasional supplementary material are given below. Page numbers indicate where the quotes, etc. appear.

1   60,000 leaving West Papua: Interview with Thom Beanal and with *Demmak*, Jayapura, April 2002.

1–2   100,000 dead: This figure is the calculation routinely quoted for those killed as a direct result of Indonesian military action in West Papua since 1962 by Amnesty International.

OPM figures and those quoted by activist networks covering the same period are as high as 300,000. A non-partisan census that would allow an accurate calculation has never been completed and the remote nature of many parts of West Papua at the time of the Dutch withdrawal meant that population figures were not available in some areas. Indonesian authorities have consistently played down figures of deaths since the 1962 transfer.

2   814,000 West Papuans at the time of the Act of Free Choice: *The Indonesian Tragedy*, Brian May, London, Routledge & Kegan Paul Ltd, 1978.

5   The two West Papuan leaders sent by Australian authorities to Manus Island were Willem Zonggonao and Clemens Runawery. See "Act of No Choice", *Dateline* (transcript), producer Mark Worth, SBS Television, 1999; and also, *Indonesia's Secret War: The Guerrilla Struggle in Irian Jaya*, Robin Osborne, Sydney, Allen & Unwin, 1985.

7–8   Death of Per-Ove Carlsson: Committee to Protect Journalists, Annual Report 1992. For more information see **www.cpj.org**.

8   "Whisky friends", Andrew Kilvert, *Inside Indonesia*, No. 61, Jan–March 2000.

20   The Indonesian Foreign Ministry now claims that direct lobbying by Indonesia did not begin at the UN until 1954. See "Revisiting the 1962 New York Terms on Papua Dupito Simamora, Indonesian Diplomat to UN, New York", *Jakarta Post*, 19 August 2002.

According to Robin Osborne the dispute predated the Indonesian nation when, in July 1945 at a meeting of the Japanese-sponsored BKPI (The Body for Researching Indonesian Independence), the majority including Sukarno voted for the inclusion of Dutch West New Guinea in the future state. *Indonesia's Secret War: The Guerrilla Struggle in Irian Jaya*, Robin Osborne, Sydney, Allen & Unwin, 1985.

21   "Historic Vote Was a Sham: Ex UN Chiefs Admit", *Sydney Morning Herald*, 23 November 2001, and on the *Associated Press Newswire* by Slobodan Lekic, Jakarta.

29–30 "Issues and Events, 2001: West Papua/Irian Jaya", Chris Ballard, *Melanesia in Review*, Canberra, Australian National University, 2001.

32–3 *Indonesian Security Responses to Resurgent Papuan Separatism: An Open Source Intelligence Case Study*, Matthew N. Davies, Canberra, Australian National University, 2001.

33   "Letter Cited as Indonesian Link to Papua Militias", Ian Timberlake, *Age*, 26 April 2002.

42   "Gas Pipeline Attack Clouds Path to Peace", Vaudine England reporting from Jakarta, *South China Morning Post*, April 2001.

44–5 Development aggression: *Observations on Human Rights Conditions in the PT Freeport Indonesia Contract of Work Areas with Recommendations*. Report prepared by Abigail Abrash, Consultant For the Robert F. Kennedy Memorial Center for Human Rights, July 2002.

47–8 Another version of these events, described in more detail, was the subject of "Blood on the Cross", *Four Corners*, produced by Mark Davis and Peter Cronau, ABC Television, 12 July 1999.

48   "The Stone Age War on Our Doorstep", Ben Bohane, *Sydney Morning Herald*, 30 December 1995.

51   *Reflections on Papua: The Future Could Be Genocide*. Report by Reverend John Barr, Executive Secretary, Unity and International Mission, Uniting Church Australian National Assembly, 10 June 2002.

51   West Papua has the highest rate of HIV in Indonesia: "Cassandra Cries for West Papua", Julie Flanagan, July 2002. TAPOL, the Indonesian Human Rights Campaign. For more information see **www.tapol.gn.apc.org**.

51   AusAID report: "PNG Faces AIDS Epidemic", *BBC News*, Asia Pacific, Tuesday, 14 May 2002.

54–5 "Appalling Violence with No Mercy in Jail Cells of Irian Jaya", Oswald Iten, *Sydney Morning Herald*, 9 January 2001.

65   *Impunity and Human Rights Violations in Papua*. Amnesty Report, April 2002. (AI Index ASA 21/015/2002)

66   *Indonesia's Secret War: The Guerrilla Struggle in Irian Jaya*, Robin Osborne, Sydney, Allen & Unwin, 1985.

67   *The Indonesian Tragedy*, Brian May, London, Routledge & Kegan Paul Ltd, 1978.

73   Appointment of Lieutenant Colonel Yayat Sudrajat to West Papua: *Reformasi: The Struggle for Power in Post-Soeharto Indonesia*, Kevin O'Rourke, Sydney, Allen & Unwin, 2002.

73 On Simbolon, Sudrajat, Hartomo: *Masters of Terror: Indonesia's Military & Violence in East Timor in 1999*, Hamish McDonald et al., Canberra, Strategic and Defence Studies Centre, Australian National University, 2002.

73–4 Lieutenant Colonel Hartomo's involvement in the Theys Eluay killing: "Problems Mount in West Papua", TAPOL press release. For more information see **www.tapol.gn.apc.org**.

74 Indonesian court acquits six former East Timor security forces officers for human rights abuses: *Associated Press Newswire*, Steve Gutkin, 21 August 2002.

74–5 Alexander Downer quote: *Associated Press Newswire*, 20 August 2002.

75 John Miller quote: US-based East Timor Action Network press release. See **www. etan.org** for more information.

75 US announcement of funding of Indonesian police force: According to Amnesty International, a police operation in the Waisor district near Manokwari in Papua throughout the second half of 2001 resulted in the detention and torture of more than 150 people. Amnesty's latest report refers to an unknown number of people who have been unlawfully killed or "disappeared" during the course of the *Brimob* operation and includes interviews with those tortured. For details of the Waisor police operation in 2001, see *Impunity and Human Rights Violations in Papua*, Amnesty Report, April 2002. (AI Index ASA 21/015/2002)

75 Sidney Jones quote: "Islamic Extremist Group Has Roots in Intelligence Operation, Report Says", Slobodan Lekic, *Associated Press Newswire*, 12 August 2002.

77–8 Rex Rumakiek: "Asia Pacific", ABC Radio, 14 August 2002.

78 "Papua New Guinea Plans Move Against Papua Rebels", *Post–Courier/PINA Nius Online*, Port Moresby, Papua New Guinea, 9 August 2002.

79 11,000 refugees on the border: *Australia's Relationhip with PNG and the Island States of the South-West Pacific*. Report submitted by the Australia West Papua Association to Senate Foreign Affairs, Defence and Trade Committee, Australian Federal Parliament, Sydney, 12 May 2002.

Kenneth Davidson

John Button's main recommendation in *Beyond Belief: What Future for Labor?* is the disaffiliation of the unions. On mature reflection I have some sympathy for this viewpoint. For far too many union leaders the union movement has become fertile territory for their political advancement, rather the advancement of their members. But there is a danger that the baby could be thrown out with the bathwater. The interests of trade unionists (and the ALP) may be better served if unionists, rather than their unions, were affiliated with the ALP. Under the present system the union secretary is able to cast a vote in Labor forums proportional to the membership or claimed membership of the union. It is the exercise of these votes, either on behalf of the union secretary personally or on behalf of the cabal with which he/she is associated – in conjunction with the state executives who control their respective ALP branches – which is the basis of the power of factional warlords.

The power of the union-based factional bosses could be curbed, and the unionists and their interests could still remain associated with the ALP in a meaningful way, if, instead of the current situation, the individual unionists were directly and individually affiliated with the ALP. Instead of bloc membership whose voting strength is exercised by the secretary of the union, unionists would be able to opt for individual membership of their industry union ALP branch or a general industry union branch in each state. The voting power of the union branch in Labor forums would be proportional to the number of unionists who explicitly opted for membership of the ALP union branch, rather than the number in the union as at present.

Should those who opt out be given a rebate equal to the individual affiliation fee with the ALP? I think not. Those who opt out would be providing more revenue for the direct operations of their union. Those who opt in are opting for more of their affiliation fee being spent on improving the general environment for unions and unionists.

Arguably, the policy of the Coalition is to make effective trade union activity illegal. For this reason there is likely to be a high proportion of unionists opting into individual affiliation with the ALP and a real focus in the industry union ALP branches on the interests of unionists, rather than on advancing the political careers of trade union officials.

But a further step is needed to break the present nexus between the position of union secretary and factional boss. Eligibility for elected office in union-based ALP branches — which would be the conduit for participation in the higher forums of the party such as State and National Conferences — would have to be restricted to union members who are not full-time office holders or paid employees of the union.

Those who would completely break the relationship between trade unions and the ALP have a duty to explain how that, in itself, would increase the power of the traditional branches and branch members of the ALP. This has not been done. The suspicion remains that the real reasons for severing the link between the trade unions and the ALP are, first, that the linkage makes the ALP less electable and, second, that breaking the link would reinforce the power of the Oligarchs who now control the party. I am cynical enough to believe that if a deal was stitched up to sever the trade union/ALP link there would be transitional arrangements put in place to protect the positions of the Oligarchs whose historic path into the oligarchy had been via the trade unions. History shows that Oligarchs never give up power voluntarily.

There are two interrelated reasons for the interest of leading Oligarchs in reforming the ALP machine. One is to reinforce their power. The quickest way to do this is to reduce the power of the trade unions movement which, for all the faults of the current system, is the only institutional mechanism through which the individuals in the existing oligarchy are likely to be disturbed.

The other is to offer the appearance or the prospect of reform in order to make the ALP under Simon Crean more electable. Trade unions are unpopular and a diminishing force, hence putting them down puts Simon Crean's electoral appeal up. The hope of reform may keep the present core of true believers inside the ALP in order to provide workers during elections. That possibility of reform might also provide a fig leaf of idealism for the ALP while the Oligarchs get on with their real business of divvying up the diminishing stock of power and patronage available to a party in opposition. And if the Oligarchs can convince the electorate that the Hawke–Wran Report[1] is serious then anything is possible at the next election.

If the Oligarchs are serious about democratic reform they must increase the power of the branches by making the branches the prime source of policy input and the pre-selection of candidates. This involves making and enforcing a few simple, understandable rules. It used to be something like this: if you were a paid-up member of the ALP for three years and you attended three meetings a year you were eligible to participate in the pre-selection process for ALP endorsement for parliamentary elections. Branch meetings had purpose because if resolutions put up in the branches got through to the State and National Conferences and were passed, they became party policy.

There is plenty of evidence that there is no will where it counts to democratise the ALP. The latest evidence is in the federal electorate of Cunningham in NSW where, as usual, the candidate for the by-election was selected by head office; and in the behaviour of the Bracks government in Victoria which has ignored a unanimous resolution of the State Conference in May 2002 to abandon its policy of encouraging expensive Public Private Partnerships in the creation of new social infrastructure. It is clear the policy is being made by the financiers who stand to profit hugely from the PPPs.

There is nothing new in this. The ALP saw early in its history that there would be an ongoing clash of interests between rank-and-file members whose interest is in advancing a set of ideas, and the paid party bureaucrats and members of parliament whose main objective would be the expansion of their power and influence through achieving government. It is a problem common to all progressive parties. The problem was put by Robert Michels, who described the dilemma from a European perspective:

> The Party, regarded as an entity ... is not necessarily identifiable with the totality of its members, and still less so with the class to which these belong. The Party is created as a means to securing an end. Having, however become an end in itself, endowed with aims and interests of its own, it undergoes a detachment from the class which it represents. In a party, it is far from obvious that the interests of the masses which have combined to form the party will coincide with the interests of the bureaucracy in which the party becomes personified.[2]

The way in which the ALP dealt with the problem is described by Vere Gordon Childe in his 1923 classic, *How Labour Governs*.[3] He outlined how and why the tripartite system of controls (Conference, Executive and Caucus) first developed in New South Wales in response to the early Labor "rats" was adopted by the other states. Childe said, "To sum up, we may say that the system of control from below adopted by the Labor Party from its inception has been proved necessary by the selfish and cowardly opportunism which has distinguished the worker's parliamentary representatives." What has changed today is that those mechanisms of control from below have been allowed to atrophy. The excuse is that the post-democratic structure of the ALP is necessary in the interests of making Labor more electable than it would be if policy is determined by the active membership.

Perhaps. But this has come at huge cost to the ALP which has been leached of most of its idealism. As Button describes it, the factions where power now resides have lost any real association with a particular ideological commitment and instead have become purely tribal. The factions' purpose now is to maximise their power in order to maximise the spoils available to their factional members.

There is no longer any serious attempt to develop policy within the party framework. The Federal Opposition dropped any pretence to a commitment to equality in education when it voted for the schools funding priorities set by the Coalition in 2001. It effectively joined the government in abandoning a commitment to Medicare as a universal system of financing health care when it announced before the election that it would not abolish the 30 per cent private health insurance rebate. The rebate had been introduced by the Coalition in order to accelerate the residualisation of public health provision, in the same way that government schools have been residualised by increasing state aid for non-government schools – financed by cuts to funding for government schools. In the lead-up to the recent election Labor goaded the government into the abolition of the automatic indexation of the petrol excise which was one of the few environmentally friendly tax measures introduced originally by the previous Labor government. The parliamentary leadership of the Labor Party is now as flexible with respect to policy developments as the Liberal Party, and policy is forged out of similarly structured focus groups.

In the longer term policy convergence on the neo-liberal grounds established by the Coalition will consign the Labor Party to irrelevance and its historic role will be taken over by some other political grouping such as the Greens or the Democrats. In this neo-liberal world there is no room for effective trade unions. As the pressure mounts on trade unions, a more purposeful leadership is likely to emerge and possibly this provides the best hope that the grip of the present oligarchy which runs the ALP can be shaken loose before the ALP dies.

I believe the true believers are necessary for the electoral success of the ALP. It was the principled stand of the true believers in 1966 which prevented the ALP accommodating the government on Australia's involvement in the war in

Vietnam and which gave the ALP a moral authority which was vital to its subsequent electoral successes in 1972 and 1975. That moral authority is now all but exhausted.

The Oligarchs must somehow be made to see that the political struggle between the left (at its best representing equality) and the right (at its best representing freedom) is built upon two incompatible economic ideologies – the one on the left representing social democracy and the control of the economy in the interests of working people, and on the right laissez faire capitalism which represents financial interests. The Oligarchs are kidding themselves if they believe there is a middle way offering security to the majority that can be built on a neo-liberal socio-economic framework.

As John Quiggin argues, "the fundamental issue of our time is whether the world will be controlled by the individual and collective actions of governments, as it was in the post-war boom under the Keynesian consensus, or by capital markets as it was in the nineteenth century."[4] The question is very open as to whether the ALP will be part of that debate in Australia. What is certain is that if it is not part of the debate, it will die.

Kenneth Davidson

1 National Committee of Review Report. August 2002. www.alp.com
2 Robert Michels, *Political Parties: A Sociological Study of the Oligarchical Tendencies of Modern Democracy*. New York: The Free Press, 1962.
3 Vere Gordon Childe, *How Labour Governs: A Study of Workers' Representation in Australia*. Melbourne: Melbourne University Press, 1964.
4 Christopher Sheil, ed., *Globalisation: Australian Impacts*. Sydney: University of NSW Press, 2001.

David Day

According to John Button, the Labor Party "is at an all-time low in its morale, ideas and democratic participation". Ironically, at the time he was writing those words, the party was occupying the government benches in every state and territory while the Liberals were almost everywhere in disarray. Only in the Federal Parliament was Labor relegated to the opposition benches. And had it not been for the Tampa "crisis" and September 11, and the fear campaign that those events allowed the conservatives to run, Labor probably would also have been on the government benches in Canberra.

Nevertheless, after three successive electoral defeats for federal Labor, it is not surprising that there should be a wide-ranging debate as to how the federal party can recover its former standing and become a serious candidate for government, particularly as the recent federal election saw an unprecedented number of staunch Labor supporters desert the party in despair, mainly over its pusillanimous response to the government's assault on asylum seekers. So some soul searching was necessary.

John Button's contribution to that debate raised many important issues, some of which have been addressed in the recent Hawke–Wran Report. One of the most interesting issues raised by John Button was that of candidate selection, which has recently seen a dramatic narrowing in the backgrounds from which candidates are drawn so that many now come from trade union offices, from within the party organisation or have worked for MPs. Few have had experience in the so-called "school of hard knocks". Not that Labor candidates were ever particularly representative of the wider society. Where, for instance, were the women or the Aboriginals? Nor does a party background necessarily preclude great candidates coming forward. John Curtin is a case in point. Perhaps more important in the temporary eclipse of federal Labor has been it partly losing sight of Chifley's "light on the hill".

In the wake of Paul Keating's unexpected electoral victory in 1993, a grand celebratory dinner was held in the great hall of Parliament House. Dubbed the "True Believers Ball", it was intended as a function to thank the hundreds of people who had combined together to thwart the apparent certainty of a Liberal victory. It had followed on from the opening remarks of Keating's acceptance speech on election night, when he had declared triumphantly that it was "a victory for the true believers". It was an unfortunate remark that was interpreted by many people as meaning that a coalition of narrow interest groups, or small cabal of ideologues, had snatched victory for themselves and would now have their snouts in the trough. The subsequent ball at Parliament House only served to confirm this impression.

Overseeing it all from the top table, in a scene reminiscent of the last supper, was a beaming Paul Keating. Down below, a rather morose-looking Bob Hawke was relegated to one of the distant long tables. Politically, the hundred-dollar-a-head dinner was a disaster, with television news cameras recording the back-slapping crowd as they trooped into the hall, dressed in their finery, to tuck into the banquet before dancing to the sound of Yothu Yindi or busily networking over the dessert and coffee. For those who caught it on the late-night news or watched it over breakfast the next morning, it would have reinforced the popular impression of politics being about "them and us", with most Australians necessarily excluded from the invitation-only celebration.

Along with Keating's exultant acceptance speech, it began to undo all the work of the election campaign, during which Labor had portrayed itself as working for all Australians while the spivs of the Liberal Party were supposedly concerned only with doing the bidding of their mates at the big end of town. The ball was a politically maladroit action by a prime minister who was exhausted by ten years in government and who was convinced that Labor had run its course on the government benches. Many of his ministers and his staff had also run out of puff and were short of ideas. Rather than seeing the unexpected 1993 victory as a chance to lay down a new agenda that might allow Keating to replicate Hawke's eight years in power, it was seen as a bonus, a chance for a last hurrah before the inevitable defeat at the next election.

Not that the Keating government squandered those last three years. Indeed, its historical significance will be seen as profound. The *Mabo* legislation and the recognition of the historic wrongs done to the indigenous peoples, the tentative moves towards a Republic and the government's embrace of Asia will continue to be seen as major achievements (even though they have been since put on hold by Howard). Yet those achievements did not lay the basis for an electoral victory by Keating in 1996. Quite the opposite. The Republic was churlishly dismissed as

Keating's Republic, with people convinced that Keating wanted to be the first president; *Mabo* was dismissed as pandering to a supposedly privileged interest group who now wanted to lay claim to suburban backyards; and the government's embrace of Asia was interpreted as surrendering Australia to Asia.

Keating had learnt his "take no prisoners" politics from Jack Lang and the men of the Labor Right in New South Wales, and his big picture politics from the grand development plans of Rex Connor. But he was deficient in the small picture, in empathising with the lives of ordinary people. Or unable or unwilling to see the world through their eyes. This was encapsulated in his offhand comment about "the recession we had to have", a remark that inspired deep and enduring resentment from the many people who were hit by high interest rates or prevented from getting work. Also, his passion for Napoleonic clocks, his part-purchase of a piggery and his mansion in Sydney all seemed to set him apart from ordinary Australians. It is one of the great ironies of recent Australian politics that this boy from the western suburbs seemed uncomfortable in the company of ordinary folk.

In contrast, John Howard deliberately depicted himself as suburban man writ small and was able to tap into the popular fears and insecurities of the suburbs, promising to make Australians relaxed and comfortable and to take politics off the front page. Of course, he has not been successful in this. Despite economic growth being high, and inflation and interest rates being low, feelings of insecurity are probably greater than they have ever been. And signs of this insecurity are mounting.

Australians who are fortunate enough to be in work are working longer and longer hours (much of it unpaid) in order to retain their jobs. (In contrast, France has introduced a thirty-five-hour week and enjoyed higher productivity as a result.) Australians who were educated in the state system are turning to private education in ever greater numbers in a costly attempt to guarantee their children a better chance in the job market and out of despair at the standards and facilities in the state system. Australians are paying ever-increasing amounts to private health insurance funds because they have lost confidence in the ability of the public health system to provide for their needs. Australians are facing ever-increasing bills for their tertiary education, with the prospect of many of them being in debt for years after graduation. Australians are enjoying longer lives but can no longer be confident of being able to fund their post-retirement years or meet their possible nursing home needs.

These insecurities were tailor-made for a strong and successful Labor campaign proposing solutions that could address the growing disparity in wealth and opportunity in Australian society. But that campaign was never mounted. Instead, the *Tampa* "crisis" allowed the government to create a new insecurity about refugees that had the effect of pushing the other insecurities back into the political shadows. And Labor found itself without an effective response, choosing instead to largely mimic the government so as to limit the electoral damage. As the man who coined the phrase "hip pocket nerve", Ben Chifley was a pragmatic politician who kept in touch with popular opinion. Yet he did not believe that basic principles were worth sacrificing for the sake of gaining or retaining power. Some elections are better lost if the price of winning them is too high. The election in November 2001 was one such election. Indeed, it might have been better for Labor's long-term success if it had retained its principles and taken the risk of losing by a landslide. (A show of political courage might even have been rewarded last November.)

Labor did not only present a weak-kneed alternative on the issue of refugees but also failed to mount any principled opposition to the government's remorseless privatisation of health and education. It could hardly do so when the Hawke and Keating governments had been complicit in those privatisations. Over the past twenty-five years, under both Labor and Liberal, society has increasingly become simply a marketplace, largely unmediated by government action, with individuals competing against each other for access to ever more limited services. It is almost as if the "greed is good" mantra of Gordon Gekko has been etched above the marbled portals of Parliament House. And, shame to say, Labor helped to hold the ladder while Howard chiselled in the words. In recent times the Labor Party has too often lost sight of its guiding principles and underlying philosophy as a social democratic party and has engaged instead in a single-minded pursuit of economic growth to satisfy the short-sighted demands of the stock market, the foreign exchange dealers and the credit agencies.

Economic issues were certainly the driving force of earlier Labor governments as well, but they had more pressing reasons for making them paramount and they were seeking different outcomes. Prime ministers such as John Curtin and Ben Chifley had grown up during the depression of the 1890s. Curtin had spent his teenage years living in squalid accommodation in Brunswick and had been forced to support his family with whatever work he could find. Chifley, who was the same age as Curtin, spent those hard years living with his grandfather on a small farm outside of Bathurst where he had the most rudimentary education at a half-time school and picked potatoes from his grandfather's paddocks. Partly as a result of these formative childhood experiences, both men were drawn into politics hoping to make a difference to the lives of ordinary people and seeking a society where capital was not king.

As late as the 1930s, Curtin still looked forward to what he called "the day of golden opportunity", when capitalism would collapse of its own accord and society could be organised in accord with the interests of ordinary people. There was passion in the politics back then, with Curtin likening himself and his Labor colleagues to "standard bearers in a holy war". Although Labor had seemed in a hopelessly divided condition after the 1931 election, Curtin kept to the task, maintaining that Labor MPs "must go on to the end and not yield while life is left to us". Which of course he did, refusing to give up the burdens of prime ministerial office in 1945 even though he knew his life was ebbing away. In his quieter way, Chifley shared that passion and that view. At the 1946 election, the former boy from the Bathurst goldfields held out a vision of Australia being on the verge of a new "golden age", with his government planning a range of nation-building measures to usher it in.

It was Menzies, after 1949, who largely got to construct that new "golden age" of full employment and unrestrained development powered by mass immigration and overseas capital. In contrast to Chifley, Menzies spoke to Australians as individuals in their homes rather than as groups in their workplaces. He spoke to them not as workers or employers but as husbands and wives, fathers and mothers. He claimed that they were the "forgotten people" whose needs would be addressed by the Liberal Party. And many of those needs were addressed by Menzies and his Liberal successors over the following twenty-three years, as they took up Chifley's vision of a "golden age" and made it their own, energetically developing and populating Australia's scattered parts. It might have gone on forever. And for those growing up during those times it seemed that Menzies and his Liberal Party were a permanent fixture on the government benches. But they gradually lost the plot. Or, rather, the plot changed.

Menzies supposed that he had given Australians what they wanted. They had their Holden cars and brick veneer houses, complete with Victa lawnmowers and Hoover washing machines, and their quarter-acre blocks were allowed to sprawl from the settled centres of the coastal cities across the former farmland to the surrounding hills. Brisbane became larger in area than London. But there was a void at the heart of these suburban sprawls. And Labor noticed it. With their houses unsewered, their roads unmade and their suburbs unconnected to public transport, with child-care non-existent and their schools over-crowded and under-funded, with universities beyond the reach of all but the wealthy and the scholarship-holders, suburban Australians were calling for government to improve the quality of their lives. Individual affluence was not enough. And Whitlam's Labor Party championed the positive role that the different levels of government could play in improving people's lives.

Whitlam also finally countered the fear-driven campaigns of the conservatives that had helped to ensure their successive electoral victories for twenty-three years. He met them head-on with courageous political initiatives that reaped big rewards, both for Labor and Australia. Rather than remaining in the shadows prior to the 1972 election, Whitlam bravely flew to Beijing and promised, if elected, to recognise the Chinese government. On Vietnam, Whitlam promised to end conscription and bring the few remaining Australian forces home. And he let Washington know that Australia would be charting a more independent course in its foreign policy. What the present crop of Labor spin doctors would have made of such initiatives can only be imagined. When Whitlam's world came crashing down with the ending of the prolonged post-war boom three years later, and Labor lost by a landslide at the 1975 election, he was still able to walk away with his reputation largely intact. Moreover, many of the more important initiatives introduced by Whitlam have endured to this day, while others such as land rights and multiculturalism were taken on board by Malcolm Fraser. His government made a lasting difference.

Now, after two decades of veneration of the market, it is time for the Labor Party to reassert the positive role that government can play in ensuring the preservation of values that we share and in shaping the sort of society that we would like to become. How can Labor accept the present wide disparity in educational outcomes in different schools (between public and private schools and even between different government schools) with the standard of facilities, teaching staff and programs depending largely on the income levels of the surrounding community rather than on the need levels of the students? Every Australian child should be able to attend a government-funded school that is the equal of their private rivals. Rather than conniving in Howard's binary system of education based on wealth, why cannot Labor return to its basic egalitarian principles and make such a commitment, promising that no Australian parent should have qualms about sending their child to the local state school. As with education, why not also with health? It would almost be worth selling the rest of Telstra if Australians could be guaranteed such achievements.

In 1945, the Labor government of John Curtin promised Australians that the devastation of the thirties depression would not be visited upon them again. Through government intervention in the economy, all those Australians who were able and wanted to work would be able to find employment. It was a commitment that was fulfilled by governments, both Labor and Liberal, for nearly thirty years thereafter, absorbing as well the millions of migrants who came to our shores during that time. How could John Curtin and Ben Chifley and Robert Menzies provide full employment for thirty years, while both Labor and Liberal parties now shrink from promising anything with regard to the unacceptably high levels of unemployment? More particularly, how can the Labor Party accept with such apparent equanimity that 20 per cent or more of our young people are unemployed? Surely the loss to our society caused by this unemployment must rank as a national disaster the equal of any flood or fire that Australia has experienced? Surely it deserves a vigorous government and private response to create work for those who want it, rather than simply blaming the victims for their plight and punishing them with bureaucratic indignities?

Howard's adroit and shameless use of the *Tampa* refugees for electoral purposes put passion back into politics, at least on the conservative side. By comparison, Labor looked grey and lifeless, as if not believing in anything. It was devoid of passion and unsure of its principles. Yet there remains much to be passionate about. More than ever, Australia has become a society of unequal chances and unequal outcomes. And despite its recent troubles, Labor remains the party best placed to address those fundamental issues of equity. After all, that was the basis of its foundation more than a hundred years ago.

David Day

Barry Jones

> I believe that [Labor voters] can have no respect for a party, certainly not
> their own party, if in a time of great national crisis, it sees no alternative
> but to carry out the policy of its opponents.
> — John Curtin, House of Representatives, 24 June 1931

This response should be seen not as a rebuttal of John Button's essay *Beyond Belief:
What Future for Labor?* but as a supplement, with some different emphases and
minor points of divergence.

Since 1929, there have been only eight changes in Federal government.
Labor has won from opposition in 1929, 1941 (in the parliament, but not at
an election), 1972 and 1983; the anti-Labor Coalition (under various names)
has regained office in 1931, 1949, 1975 and 1996. Winning from opposition
is tough — and rare.

How Important Are Structural Issues?

Following Whitlam's heavy defeat in 1977, Bill Hayden set up an ALP National
Committee of Enquiry (1978), chaired by John Button, with Hawke and Hayden
among its members. It was critical about party structures and made sweeping
recommendations, essentially to abandon "the Federal Principle" — that the party
should operate as a national entity organised on national lines, not just as a coalition of states as it had been in 1902. Few of its recommendations were adopted.
Despite this discouraging response, five years later under Bob Hawke, Labor won
election with a comfortable majority. The party has shown remarkable resilience
in the past, and may well bounce back again.

After the 2001 defeat, Simon Crean set up a National Committee of Review,
consisting of Bob Hawke and Neville Wran, with terms of reference remarkably
similar to the Button Enquiry of 1978. Both John Button and I made written
submissions to the review. Its report was published in August.

While their thirty-eight recommendations are essentially about the ALP's composition and structure, the Hawke–Wran Report must be read in a broad political context. In their extensive meetings with rank-and-file party members throughout Australia, Hawke and Wran were impressed by a passionate commitment to change. ALP members want "bottom up" processes to replace the current system of "democratic centralism" where head office, factional leaders and, perhaps, spin doctors make all the important decisions about how the party operates, policy directions and choice of candidates.

They emphasise that the party must have a strong commitment to:

— the collective responsibility of society (i.e. not leaving everything to the market)
— unqualified opposition to discrimination of all kinds
— recognition of Aboriginal prior ownership of the continent
— an independent foreign policy
— protection of the natural environment (I would have added, cultural)
— an enlarged population, including more genuine refugees
— the right of workers to organise and bargain collectively
— "a correct and humane policy" for boat people and refugees, and
— overcoming "a perceived lack of policy differentiation from our conservative opponents".

On party structure, Hawke–Wran attack "the deadening impact of factionalism and the associated phenomenon of branch-stacking" and "the cancerous effect this activity has had on the democratic traditions that have been the strength of our Party". I agree with Button/Hawke–Wran in their concerns about the impact of factionalism, branch-stacking and its "cancerous effect" on the democratic traditions of the party. Simon Crean has been courageous in pursuing organisation restructure and deserves full support.

Nevertheless, there are some unexamined paradoxes in both documents. I support the much discussed move from 60–40 trades unions share of delegates at ALP Conferences to 50–50 and taking strong action against branch-stacking and factional excesses, but these issues may be of minor importance to Labor voters.

Both Button (p. 27) and Hawke–Wran (p. 15) refer to the case of *Clarke v. the South Australian ALP*, in which the South Australian Supreme Court made an adverse judgement on "vigorous recruitment", leading to the displacement of a long serving MP, Ralph Clarke. Clarke then contested his own seat as an Independent.

Did disaffected voters rise in righteous indignation to re-elect Clarke? No, they did not. I conclude that filling the policy vacuum, showing leadership and getting away from convergence mode is far more important.

Another paradox is: if the diagnosis of pathology in the ALP's body politic is correct, why is it only crippling at the federal level? Labor holds office in every state and territory, facing extraordinarily weak opposition. The State Liberal Parliamentary Parties are in disarray in Victoria, Queensland and Tasmania, and in poor shape in New South Wales, South Australia and Western Australia. This is curious, because Labor's aspirations are national, despite the creaking federal structure of its organisation.

In the Commonwealth, the Coalition is ascendant and the Labor Opposition is going through a painful process of restructuring. In each state and territory, the ALP Premier or Chief Minister is a popular figure, well ahead of the Opposition Leader, and they are perceived as competent managers/administrators. State government is essentially regarded as being about housekeeping, not the generation of new policy directions.

New policy directions, setting a national vision, is seen as the role of the Commonwealth government – and this is where federal Labor appears at a distinct disadvantage. Polling for our State Parliamentary Parties appears to be significantly higher than for the Federal Parliamentary Party.

Adopting the Hawke–Wran Report will not only be good for the ALP but should make a vital contribution to raising the level of national political debate, restoring a moral and intellectual agenda in elections, reviving a sense of community and the legitimacy of democratic processes.

There are some significant weaknesses – on affirmative action and indigenous representation – and proposals to create special interest branches will need careful monitoring to avoid rorting. Hawke–Wran worry about the policy vacuum but make no reference to Knowledge Nation.

I agree with Hawke–Wran on changing 60–40 union representation at Conferences to 50–50 and agree that trades unions should be encouraged to play active roles in the ALP. I disagree with John Button's view that the time "for a friendly divorce" might have come, although he is correct to point out that "unions affiliated with the ALP represent less than 15 per cent of the workforce" (p. 37) and contribute only 24 per cent of the ALP's income.

There are two objections to changing 60–40: the property argument ("It's our property isn't it, and why should we give anything up?") and the nostalgia argument ("Unions founded the show in 1891 and nothing much has changed in Australia since then").

Labor's "Small Target" Strategy: The Convergence Problem

The "small target" strategy Labor adopted for the 2001 election was completely misconceived – a suspension of belief which resulted from over-reliance on spin doctors and reports from focus groups. As John Button points out (p. 10) it was an adaptation of John Howard's successful "relaxed and comfortable" strategy in 1996, with echoes of A.A. Milne's Christopher Robin in *Vespers* ("If I curl up small, nobody will know that I'm there at all"). It was hard to imagine Kim Beazley curling up small.

The 1998 election had been largely fought on the GST – and Labor polled far better than it expected, or deserved. Kim Beazley's advisors thought the 2001 election would be fought, once more, on the GST, and starting, as we did, on a higher baseline than in 1998 there would be sufficient community aggravation about the tax for Labor to win. The strategy was to avoid confrontation with the government on any issue other than GST. Labor voted for government legislation in the Senate which weakened Medicare and state schools for fear of creating a row and offending "aspirational voters". This angered many "true believers".

It proved to be a monumental miscalculation. The GST was a key issue in 1998 and changed many votes – but by 2001 the GST, however unpopular, had been accepted as a fact of life. Labor's "Rollback" policy, proposing to remove the GST from a few classes of goods, was seen as merely tinkering at the margins. Button calls it "pathetic, feeble, vague, cynical, hypocritical". It was even worse. Five Labor state premiers lacked enthusiasm for prejudicing their guaranteed income stream from the GST. Australians are pragmatic and, however much they might have grumbled about the GST and the cost and time involved in making quarterly returns, they were never going to switch their votes on a dead issue.

In the 1980s Labor, in office, moved steadily to the right, and the Coalition went even further. This was the time that the politics went out of politics, marked by the death of ideology, the rise and rise of economics as a dominant paradigm, the commercialisation of values, and replacement of community values by the market.

By 2001, both parties assumed that the electorate would make only conservative, self-serving judgements on personal taxation and levels of government spending. Thus, it was felt, appeals to vision and the long term could be disregarded. This was a completely untested hypothesis. One issue that the ALP did not poll on was this: "Since the electorate was prepared to support temporary levies to pay for the guns buy-back scheme and military intervention in East Timor, would voters be prepared to pay higher taxes if they were targeted to particular problems in health, education, employment and the environment?"

In the UK, polls carried out by *The Economist* found that 70 per cent of taxpayers said they would pay more tax if they believed the community would get value for money – but no polling organisation has asked Australian taxpayers on this issue.

On defence and foreign policy issues, Labor and the Coalition appeared to be dancing the tango – if the Prime Minister moved, Labor followed. It was as if Howard had said to Beazley, "I don't think that Reconciliation and the Republic should be election issues," and Kim had said, "Thank you. We agree."

The high degree of convergence involved in the "small target" strategy had two results – first, it alienated many voters of even vaguely radical persuasion and made the Greens and even the Democrats seem attractive for a first preference vote, second, it put an exaggerated emphasis on the role of the leaders. There was a reduction in the tribal appeal of voting Labor or Liberal – the main question became: "In dangerous times, who is the stronger leader?" Paradoxically, Howard's apparent lack of personal charisma operated in his favour, with the Liberal sub-text: "You don't have to like John Howard to know that he is a gutsy, tough little fighter, dogged and persistent. Like him or not, you know where you are with him." There was a disconnect between "liking" and (grudging) "support".

In practice, there is a higher degree of convergence on major policies between parliamentary parties than there is between activists in party branches. (This is contrary to the conventional wisdom that parliament is a bear pit.) Labor branch activists tend to be to the left of the ALP's parliamentary leadership, Liberal activists further to the right, National Party activists further right again, and Democrat branch members much further to the left of their senators.

Leadership

Kim Beazley was probably the ALP's most conservative federal leader – certainly since J.H. Scullin. Malcolm Fraser says, "I have only one problem with Kim Beazley. I can't think of a single issue where he is to the Left of me."

He was not a "change agent" – and I doubt if he saw himself as such. That made his establishment of the Knowledge Nation Task Force, under my chairmanship, such an anomaly – because if the Task Force proposed major policy commitments, as it did, they either had to be adopted or rejected. Sadly, Kim did both, accepting the report in its entirety, pledging himself to its adoption, only to be persuaded to walk away as soon as it came under attack.

Kim Beazley's moving concession speech on election night suggested how a moral argument might have been advanced in the campaign. He said, "There are dark angels in our nature but there are good angels as well." He was probably reaching out for Lincoln's reference to "the better angels of our nature". Despite all this, it is possible to propound an optimistic view of the 2001 election. (There were hard-nosed ALP strategists who kept insisting, privately, that Labor would win, until the Thursday before polling day.)

The optimistic view is that, considering the appalling political impact of the asylum seekers crisis, the September 11 terrorist attack in the US and the war in Afghanistan in the weeks leading up to election day, the final result was relatively close, with the ALP gaining 49.5 per cent of the two-party preferred votes after all preferences from minor parties had been distributed. The Coalition won a majority of twelve seats in 1998 in an election fought on the GST; unpopular for Howard, good for Beazley. In 2001 (with the House increased from 148 to 151 members) the Coalition's majority only increased to thirteen seats (but with the support of several Independents). Kim Beazley was regarded as having won the three set-piece engagements of the 2001 campaign – the debate with John Howard, the Policy Launches and the National Press Club speeches. Labor's election advertising was generally more effective. From that perspective, Labor's "small target" strategy of remaining virtually invisible until a few weeks before polling day might be considered to have been surprisingly successful – and, if three voters in every 200 had changed, a winning strategy.

The pessimistic view is that Labor's primary vote has fallen to its lowest figure (38.2 per cent) since 1934. The 1998 election result provided a false optimism because it was fought on an issue (GST) that suited Labor. There is serious questioning in the ALP about an apparent policy vacuum. The ALP has, for practical purposes, become a party of the centre right. Is there room for a mainstream party of the left in Australia? Many Labor supporters felt alienated from the official line on the refugees, defected to cast primary votes for Greens or Democrats in the House of Representatives, but gave Labor their effective preference votes. But this could change. This raises serious debate about whether the party is essentially the political expression of the trade union movement, or a broad coalition of all citizens who believe that humane, social values are more important than market values. Many traditional Labor voters disliked the "small target" approach and felt that the party had gone missing on many major issues such as education, health, the environment and immigration since Keating's defeat in 1996.

Wedge Politics

John Howard is a strong and successful practitioner of "wedge politics", a concept developed in the US by Nixon, Reagan and the senior Bush, in which the major dividing line in society is not between left and right (terms that have become increasingly meaningless since the collapse of the Soviet Union), rich and poor, but between elite opinion and popular opinion, with a deeply anti-intellectual emphasis (= dumbing down).

Howard pushes a strongly elitist *economic* agenda but a strongly populist *social* agenda. He is also a "conviction" politician, prepared to push ahead on issues which were, on the face of it, vote losers, such as the GST and selling off Telstra. But he pushes ahead – and wins. On balance, I think he will succeed in selling off Telstra. One of his strongest attributes is when he says, "You mightn't like what I am doing, but you know where I stand."

In 2001 he succeeded in destroying the One Nation Party electorally, but adopted much of its agenda and secured much of its vote. Labor seemed to be a passive, but appalled, onlooker.

The hard men in both Labor and the Coalition convinced themselves that winning the election depended on how strongly Howard and Beazley succeeded in projecting a tough line against refugees. John Howard won this contest convincingly, conveying the impression that Australia was at risk from the boat people, demonising the victims, depriving them of access to the protection of our legal system, and dropping in the inflammatory suggestion of a possible link between asylum seekers and terrorists. They were an amorphous, but threatening, mass – without names, faces or individuality.

Beazley protested that he was just as hardline as Howard on refugees and border protection, but many voters were unconvinced. They knew Howard meant it – it was consistent with his uncompromising line on Reconciliation, but they weren't sure about Beazley. Could he really mean it? I suspect that he was closer to Howard on refugees than many thought, while deploring the inflammatory language and the use of coded appeals to racism.

The whole political process – not just Labor – was locked into two rigidities:

— That every Budget must be in surplus, whatever the circumstances, and if not, then the whole economy is threatened. (Ross Gittins roundly attacked this in the *Age* and the *Sydney Morning Herald* as "rubbish". In our own lives, we recognise that major investments – such as a house or car purchase – cannot be met from current account.) The 2002 Federal Budget blew this orthodoxy out of the water.

— That Australia's security was at risk from invading boat people – and that there was an absolute upper limit for refugees of 12,000 per annum. (Under Malcolm Fraser there was a 100,000 intake after the Vietnam War, and Bob Hawke allowed 20,000 Chinese students to stay after the

Tiananmen Square massacre in 1989.) In reality, the number of "illegals" was about 4,000.

John Howard was masterful in emphasising immediate self-interest, emphasising the familiar, the obvious, the short-term, and discounting or ridiculing complex, long-term issues requiring intellectual input – such as constitutional reform, Reconciliation, the Republic, Knowledge Nation, the environment or appropriate future population levels. "What's in it for you and your family?" may be a useful tactical approach, but strategically it is bankrupt.

Unfortunately, the word "values" was never used in the campaign. Labor conveyed neither vision or courage – witness the sidelining of Knowledge Nation, and the major issues, such as soil and water, population, and ageing that were central to it.

Filling the Policy Vacuum

Since 1996, the major effects of the Howard government's policies have been to:

1 Cripple trades unions and diminish an important countervailing force
2 Weaken the industrial arbitration system
3 Widen the gap between rich and poor
4 Lower minimum wages (but end any caps on high salaries)
5 Marginalise Australia's egalitarian ethos
6 Subsidise private medical insurance and weaken Medicare ("choice")
7 Subsidise private schools and impoverish state schools ("choice")
8 Reduce the CSIRO's capacity
9 Damage the ABC and Radio Australia
10 Hollow out universities and convert them to trading corporations (emphasising application rather than knowledge)
11 Adopt a punitive approach to Aboriginals – reject apology and cut back on native title
12 Disregard environmental challenges (Greenhouse, salination, deforestation)
13 Repudiate affirmative action and weaken women's rights
14 Denigrate multiculturalism
15 Promote the cult of mediocrity
16 Punish the unemployed
17 Derail moves towards a Republic
18 Punish refugees

19 Repudiate international criticism (e.g. the UN on human rights)
20 Turn a blind eye to our history. We are into the politics of denial ("it never happened"), amnesia ("I don't know anything about it; it was before my time") and nostalgia ("It was better in the old days")
21 Treat drug use as a criminal problem, not a social and medical one
22 Use the GST to move tax burdens downwards
23 Strengthen corporate power
24 Sell off Telstra
25 Politicise the High Court by selecting overtly "big C" Conservative judges (Mason, Deane, Brennan and Wilson were all appointees of previous Coalition governments, but would not have been Howard's choices)
26 Reduce public service expertise and independence, insisting that there are no policy problems in health, education, research, media or the environment, only *management* problems
27 Put senior public service staff on contract, thus reducing the collective memory, with re-appointment dependent on telling the government what it wants to hear, instead of providing "frank and fearless" advice
28 Make ideological decisions that the market always knows best, all values have a dollar equivalent, a privatised service is always better than a state-run one (e.g. health, education, transport, communications, detention centres)
29 Maintain the conviction that Australia's economy is essentially based on primary production (i.e. that it remains an "Old" economy)
30 Downgrade the concept of "the public good", promoting "the private good" (self-interest).

Reversing the thirty changes set out above must be the core of a coherent Labor policy. Few of them were raised during the 2001 campaign, or in parliament between 1996 and 2001.

Knowledge Nation

John Button wrote (p. 12):

> "Knowledge Nation", a vision for a better educated society – which properly refined and packaged in terms of its significance might have been a [policy?] centrepiece – was announced and then backed away from, largely because of its easily mocked spaghetti

and meatballs diagram. This was all small target stuff, which made it difficult to explain what the Opposition believed.

This summary represents a widely held view that Knowledge Nation, was essentially about schools, universities and TAFE. It was far broader.

The Knowledge Nation Task Force Report was a comprehensive policy framework linking those elements in Australia's society, economy and environment, especially human and physical resources, which depend on the generation, use and exchange of knowledge. Education was a central part of it – but the thrust of our report emphasised the importance of linkages, and the nature of complex systems.

I chaired an impressive task force of twenty-two professionals, fourteen of them experts from outside the party in a variety of areas – medicine, banking, electronics, teaching, economics, trade and international affairs. Most members had been used by governments on both sides of politics. Peter Doherty, Gus Nossal, Don Lamberton and Peter Karmel were among many outsiders who also made valuable suggestions for the task force. We concluded that much important knowledge is locked up in silos and national linkages tend to be very weak, compounded by the dispersal of population across a huge continent.

The number one priority in Knowledge Nation was a "massive ten-year program to tackle major problems which threatened the nation's viability, especially in regional and remote areas, such as desertification, soil salinity and acidification, pollution of rivers and erosion, coordinating the efforts of all research organisations, bringing the cities and the bush together". In part, Knowledge Nation followed up on a major report on land degradation by the National Farmers' Federation (NFF) and the Australian Conservation Foundation (ACF), *National Investment in Rural Landscapes* (May 2000). This estimated the cost of combating salinity and restoring the land at $65 billion and proposed a $37 billion program of government assistance over ten years. Other sources suggested higher figures. The House of Representatives Committee on Environment and Heritage, chaired by Ian Causley, MP, conducted an Inquiry into Catchment Management. Its unanimous report (December 2000) came to similar conclusions as the NFF–ACF and recommended that the government impose an environmental levy to meet the cost of restoring soil and water. We hoped that bipartisan support would be guaranteed on this vital issue.

Not one media outlet reported this, Labor never referred to it again, and we scored an own goal. Reporting on Knowledge Nation was very narrow and selective. Commentators concentrated on their areas of interest or concern to the exclusion of everything else. Some saw the document as Labor's science policy, research and development policy, still more as its education policy.

When the report was released on 2 July, the government decided on a direct hit strategy. This was in striking contrast to Labor's general support for the government's Backing Australia's Ability program, and the Prime Minister's speech on 29 January 2001 launching it. The government singled out two elements for attack, and the attack then became the story, not the report's contents.

First was my notorious "Complexity diagram", demonstrating dynamic linkages between systems, first mocked as "spaghetti and meatballs" by David Kemp, the Education Minister, and as "Noodle Nation" by Treasurer Peter Costello. Kemp, as a certified intellectual, knew better; Costello may not have. This ridicule was then taken up enthusiastically by the media, particularly the *Australian*.

Second was the suggested use of the term "Cadastre" as a provisional, shorthand description for a proposed comprehensive national "Knowledge Bank" to provide a picture of our physical, social and economic condition, indicating strengths and weaknesses in our skills base. This seemed to enrage some commentators.

We were arguing that policies such as health and education and social welfare and environment have a complex and dynamic interaction: touch one, and the others are all affected. They are not wrapped up discretely, like Christmas presents. Young people, familiar with mind maps, understood the diagram; journalists and politicians did not. To many journalists, columnists and cartoonists, the diagram was the beginning and the end of discussion. The basic objection seemed to be: "It's all too complex". But Australia faces complex times with complex issues. As H.L. Mencken observed, "For every complex problem there is a simple solution, and it is almost always wrong."

Media failure to examine and analyse Knowledge Nation was a major disgrace. In the print media, no one recognised its interconnectedness, the heavy emphasis on the environment, on the creative arts, on a national population policy, on demographic changes and the significance of the "Third Age", a national information policy, getting more effective co-ordination in our research institutions, a strategic approach to concentration on research and industry priorities, the emphasis on values, changing the culture, strengthening great national institutions such as the ABC and the CSIRO, getting away from a narrow materialist instrumentalism (digging deeper furrows) in education, and redefining the role of government. Some writers automatically assumed that Knowledge Nation proposed a revival of "big government", and ignored our careful attempt to limit and redefine its appropriate role. The advice of the party's spin doctors was simply to ignore the attacks on Knowledge Nation, and let the issue drift for a month or two.

It was a serious misjudgment. By 4 July, Knowledge Nation was essentially dead in the water and the Opposition seemed to have taken a vow of silence.

The 2001 election was, I believe, effectively lost after the Aston by-election on 14 July. Knowledge Nation simply disappeared in that mini-campaign, although it could have been used effectively. We failed to secure Green preferences because the ALP negotiator was unaware that Knowledge Nation had an environment component; indeed, that it was central.

To my knowledge, there never was a briefing on Knowledge Nation for head office, shadow cabinet, caucus, state branches or candidates. The report's first print run was 300 copies. Ultimately 1,000 copies were printed for Australia-wide distribution. However, there was no strategy for getting material out to trades unions, schools, universities, TAFEs or community groups and providing follow-up. While the material was available on the ALP's website, it scored only 4,369 "hits", so few voters were familiar with it. Some shadow ministers failed to connect their policy responsibilities with Knowledge Nation. There was no attempt to brief the press gallery effectively to counteract initial skepticism about Knowledge Nation, or to talk, even generally, about potential cost.

The central problem with Labor's approach to Knowledge Nation strategy is that it was impossible to reconcile the report with the "small target", no/low spending Budget strategy (with the repeated mantra about no Budget deficits), the general approach of avoiding controversy on policy (e.g. education and health) and fighting essentially on terrains chosen by the government.

Offers of help from Professor Peter Doherty, Dr Tim Flannery, Professor Fiona Stanley, Peter Verwer (CEO of the Property Council of Australia), Leith Boully (grazier and member of the ABC Board) and others were not followed up.

Kim Beazley never talked about the "soil and water" emphasis in Knowledge Nation. Perhaps his advisors took the line that proposing "a massive ten year program" (our words) could only be categorised as major expenditure. If he was then challenged about a spending commitment and said, "But we will only spend, year by year, what the Budget surplus allows," then the credibility of the "massive program" would have been shot.

There was a re-launch of Knowledge Nation at Berwick (in the marginal seat of La Trobe) at a large meeting addressed by Kim Beazley, Steve Bracks and myself, accompanied by a glossy pamphlet: "What I Stand For", striking for its vagueness and parsimony, which was to be circulated nationally. In the pamphlet, only two specific spending promises were made: "Allocate $100 million to improve class-rooms, libraries and laboratories [in schools]" and "Spend $148 million in its first three years of government to mount a fight against cancer." KNOWLEDGE

NATION, in capitals, appeared on only one page. The impression was given that Knowledge Nation was entirely about education and training. Labor promised "Ending the university and TAFE funding crisis", but no costings were offered.

The timing of the Berwick re-launch was unfortunate: 11 September.

Understandably, Kim Beazley's speech was unreported and the pamphlet disappeared from sight. I was amazed that the party used the name "Kim Beazley's Knowledge Nation" as the centrepiece of Kim's election policy launch in Hurstville on Wednesday, 31 October (just nine days before the election).

The document *Kim Beazley's Plan for the Knowledge Nation* bears little resemblance to the Task Force Report, confining itself to proposing modest increases in education-spending over five years. Oddly, in a table headed "Value of Labor's Commitment to the Knowledge Nation", projected expenditure for the Knowledge Bank (a.k.a Cadastre), a central feature of the Task Force Report, was listed as $0 – spread over five years!

Labor must be prepared to tackle complex issues. Knowledge Nation was far less complex than Howard's GST proposal – an issue that he won on despite its perceived unpopularity. Gough Whitlam's "Platform" was varied and complex – and had to be explained, over and over again, for five years before Labor won in 1972. This is the only way to get new ideas up on the agenda.

In the 1992 Curtin Lecture in Perth I distinguished between "spectrum issues" and "litmus issues". Spectrum issues are those which nobody disagrees with. Nobody opposes job creation, better education or better health. The policy divide is on how best to tackle them, and which ranks first, second or third in priority. The issue is always which party or operating method is likely to bring about a better outcome.

The ALP's 2001 election slogan: "Jobs. Education. Health" was not a vote changer. Litmus issues, which involve "Yes" or "No" responses, are vote changers – as Whitlam proved in 1972 (and even 1969) – recognising the PRC, ending Conscription, abolishing the death penalty etc. "Put State Schools first" or "Raise the Medibank levy" would have been litmus issues. When Kim raised elements of Knowledge Nation in the last nine days before the election they seemed like spectrum (or motherhood?) issues.

60–40? or 3+2?

The great task for Labor is to unite two major groups – traditional blue collar workers and their families, and progressive professionals. It can be done but it will require more heavy lifting on policy matters than was shown at the three last National Conferences. Some of Labor's most visionary leaders, notably Ben

Chifley, came from impeccably blue collar backgrounds – but they wanted to be change agents and he had breadth, depth and courage.

The ALP needs 5 million votes to win a federal election comfortably. The trades unions may be able to pull in 2 million of those votes – and maintaining their commitment to Labor is essential. Is this support dependent on maintaining the 60–40 rule, that trades union delegates are to have 60 per cent of representation at State Conferences? Some trades union leaders say "Yes" – and that is hardly surprising. So do the powerbrokers who currently run state ALP branches. It would be amazing (and unselfish) if they questioned the operation of a system that puts – and maintains – them where they are.

But insufficient attention has been given to the 3,000,000 non trades unionists whose votes we must have to win. Where do they fit in?

Labor needs both. If the ALP holds the 2 million and loses the 3 million then the Coalition wins overwhelmingly. If we hold the 3 million and lose the 2 million then the result would be almost as bad.

The question of the 60–40 relationship between trades union and branch representation at State Conferences may be a second order issue. There is little empirical evidence that it is a major factor deterring voters from supporting Labor. In the context of factional control of the party, where the Left has fragmented and no longer offers an effective countervailing force to the Right, a change from 60–40 to 50–50 (or even a return to 70–30) will not necessarily change how the party operates.

The 60–40 rule has more symbolic significance than substance. It enables trades union officials to feel that they retain ownership of the party and its policies. In reality this is not the case, and has not been for twenty years. At successive recent National Conferences, the ACTU and affiliated unions have had a record of being gracious in defeat. It is hard to point to a single issue where, in the end, the trades unions have won the day against the political leadership. (Defeat of the "fair trade" proposition put by trades unions at the Hobart Conference in 2002 demonstrates this.)

Paradoxically, the tradition of gracious defeat makes the 60–40 rule such an important symbol. Some trades union leaders feel that having lost the *substance* of control, they can't afford to give up the *symbolism* as well.

The more serious question at the core of the 3+2 problem is whether it is possible to build a dynamic and expanding party on a contracting base. If so, how? The historic turning point for trades union membership as a percentage of the total labour force was 1954. That year was the high point. For forty-eight years it has persistently declined. (Which is starting to look like a trend.)

This reflects the changing nature of the work force. Contracting employment sectors remain highly unionised, while expanding employment sectors are barely unionised at all. Society has changed since Labor's foundation in 1891. Should our party structure reflect existing society, or society as it was?

In November 1999, National Secretary Gary Gray provided a table to the ALP National Executive which indicated that nationally affiliated union members fell from 1,710,000 in 1990 to 1,133,000 in 1999. The numbers have stabilised since then, but the percentage is still falling.

If we assume that 80 per cent of affiliated trades unionists vote for the ALP (probably too high since the ALP primary vote in highly industrialised, and therefore unionised, federal seats nowhere exceeds 70 per cent), this gives a figure of 906,000. Most families involved in trades unions will include partners and children who are members themselves, so calculating a multiplier is difficult. Applying a generous multiplier of 2.2 gives a base of 2 million voters – barely 40 per cent of the votes Labor needs to govern federally.

What model of Australia are we appealing to? Nostalgia has its value, but the ALP cannot simply be a heritage party.

Trades union representation at State and National Conferences is essentially a top down affair – deals are stitched up by the factions that run the unions. It is far from clear how far union delegates reflect the views of rank-and-file workers on non-industrial issues. The SDA (Shop Distributive and Allied Employees' Association), which claims to speak for a young, largely female, labour force, argues a hardline position on moral issues, including opposition to abortion and stem-cell research. Are these views shared by shop assistants throughout Australia? Have the issues been put to them for debate? I cannot recall any salesperson, male or female, ever urging me to support the moral agenda of the SDA.

Factionalism and "Democratic Centralism"

The party cannot win elections without an alliance between the 2 million trade unionists and those 3 million voters who are sympathetic to change. These 3 million must be encouraged to become involved. The present "top down" power structure depends to a large extent on keeping branch membership low, inactive and ageing, because factionalism is easier to organise and impose on a small membership base. It is a safe generalisation that factional strength has an inverse relationship to the numbers of people involved. It is absolutely decisive with the 200 National Conference delegates. It has no impact, other than varying degrees of distaste, with the 5 million potential Labor voters. Button comments on the *apparatchiki* who run factions that "as public figures they are about as attractive as Hannibal Lecter".

Factionalism proved to be a useful instrument for dispute resolution in the Hawke–Keating years and contributed to the stability of caucus during a thirteen-year period. However, in opposition, factions tend to become mere recruiting agencies and have a life of their own. Candidates are pre-selected on the basis of loyalty to the faction, rather than – say – a high level of community involvement.

Any recommendation to limit factional power, or prohibit branch-stacking ("vigorous recruiting") will be hard to enforce because many existing officials have been beneficiaries of past practice. Some attempt should be made to provide opportunities for branch members to feel that they have an ownership stake in the National Conference.

I recommended a major reform to Hawke–Wran to involve the 3+2. I proposed direct election by party members, including trades unionists who actually held a party ticket, for National President, National Secretary, 151 conference delegates (= one for each federal electorate), and Senate candidates.

Excessive factionalism has led to endorsing weak or compliant federal and state candidates. It is hard to identify any recent recruit to the Senate who has not been either a trade union official, a party office official, a ministerial staffer, a parliamentary staffer, a factional organisor, or has strong family linkages or sub-factional alliances.

Human cloning may be with us already!

Barry Jones

Susan Ryan

All of us interested, for whatever reason, in the possibility of the ALP's regeneration should thank John Button. His long essay *Beyond Belief* documents and examines those many aspects of structure and performance that, left unchanged, will continue to block Labor from winning another federal election. In a fluent and resonant narrative, Button brings to bear a lifetime's experience of the party machine and of Government and Opposition. A wide-ranging, highly informed account, it is enlivened by his sharp insights into the broader Australian community, which he has long observed with wry affection.

Button's version of where Labor is and how it got there is all the more engaging because of his writer's eye for ironic detail. I didn't remember the items on the menu at the True Believers' celebratory centenary dinner in May 2001. Button reminds us that this event was our last great moment of pride before the fall. Signals of the imminence of the fall resided perhaps, on that faraway happy evening, as much in the style of the repast as in the presentations of the stellar array of party leaders. Did only Button notice? Later, with a couple of precise anecdotes, he gives voice to Labor's forgotten people, the ordinary branch members. His few words about one branch meeting and a chance conversation with two longstanding but disappointed locals say it all, perhaps better than the thirty-eight detailed and exhaustive recommendations of the Hawke–Wran Report.

It is useful that Button puts the debate in an international context. The current dangerous public argument about the optimal relationship between the ALP organisation and the unions could have started and gone on more fruitfully. A careful look at different versions of the way labour-oriented parties and unions work together in Scandinavian countries and Germany might have helped Simon Crean renovate this crucial but tangled relationship. Unlike Button, though, I can't see that the time is right for a big change. A proposal for a European-style separate co-operative model is unlikely to gain acceptance here, from either partner. Starting from an international perspective, however, this important discussion might have kept a more reasonable tone, and Crean's sincere efforts might have met with less media coverage and more internal success.

New Zealand Labour's triumphs, despite or because of truly opening up to women at all levels including the prime ministership, show up the ALP's clumsy, grudging and still ambivalent approach to gender equality within the party for what it is: another outcome of faction power, which has always been, and remains, exclusively male power.

There is no more telling example of how factionalism distorts and destroys progressive developments than what has happened to Labor women as they have increased their numbers in the Federal Parliament. John Button refers to this, and I will expand his point.

Since the election of 1975, when I joined two other Labor women in parliament (Senators Ruth Coleman and Jean Melzer), female numbers have grown, if slowly, so that now women are nearly one-third of the federal caucus, that is, twenty-nine of the ninety-three members are women. At first this change was almost solely the result of Labor women's own efforts. Against a history of exclusion we fought to get on to party committees, to be heard in party forums, to insist that equal pay, anti-discrimination laws, equal access to education and training and government-funded child care got onto the main agenda. Women planned and organised pre-selections, flying in the face of Labor tradition and more often than not putting up with male derision and obstruction.

The wider social change throughout Australia, of which these actions were partly a result and partly a cause, meant that more women felt confident to attempt the challenges. More men saw the justice, and perhaps the electoral advantage, of supporting female candidates.

In policy outcomes, leading up to and following the election of the Hawke government in March 1983, the presence of these women, and the pro-women policies they helped design, were vindicated. Labor attracted more electoral support from women than ever before, getting, for the first time, over 50 per cent of the female vote and closing the gender gap, the historic gap between female and male support for Labor.

These improvements endured for a few years, during which Labor enacted a raft of anti-discrimination and equal opportunity laws in support of women, and introduced policies across the board aimed at removing past discrimination and providing fairer access to all important programs and services. Some excellent and emblematic appointments were made: Mary Gaudron to the High Court, Helen Williams as the first female head of a government department, as well as other capable women to statutory bodies and agencies.

When the last decade of the twentieth century arrived, this forward movement stalled. Experienced and effective women within the party grew impatient with the slowing of progress, particularly with the continued bias against selecting female candidates. They sought and got an affirmative action rule that requires the party to achieve 35 per cent of female candidates in winnable seats in all elections. This goal was to have been achieved by this year, 2002. Overall, Labor has got close. The rule and the support group it generated, Emily's List, headed by former premier Joan Kirner, has helped to grow the female numbers over the last few years. As well, the rule has kept visible in the party and the media the objective of gender equality, and Labor's performance in relation to it.

The potential electoral and policy benefits of these modest successes have been thwarted by the continued stranglehold on the parliamentary party of the male-run factions. The increased presence of women in caucus has produced little new policy or legislation to address the continuing disadvantages experienced by women, be they young mothers struggling to support their children in an unfriendly labour market, or older women left behind by patchy superannuation arrangements. Nor has this enhanced female presence been perceived by the electorate to have changed the discriminatory male thinking and culture of Labor.

Once the affirmative action rule came in, the factions, pragmatically, set about manipulating it to secure their own advantage. They would now have to put up with female candidates, so they would choose women from their own faction. Those women, if successful, would be beholden to their faction and provide more reliable numbers. And that is how the rule has played out. There are more female MPs but they have not produced better public positions on refugees, private health insurance or schools funding policy. How was it, with all those Labor women in the Federal Parliament last election, the best offer that Beazley could come up with was taking the GST off tampons? Are all the women currently in caucus happy with Crean's adherence to mandatory detention for asylum seekers? If not, how can the electorate tell?

Just as destructive as the factions' stranglehold on policy and their female members is their willingness to do deals with each other on pre-selections. A few years ago, in an unusually lively Sydney branch (non-stacked), we had the opportunity to vote in a pre-selection for a state candidate. Our branch, which contained quite a few of John Button's "new believers", produced a strong candidate – a mature, left-wing woman who was well known, respected and active in many community organisations, with a long and impressive track record in supporting the party and numerous candidates, state and federal. Her strengths matched the electorate's needs and interests. Our branch was advised that this candidate could not succeed. Those-who-must-be-obeyed had already agreed on the candidate – a right-wing male who by no objective assessment was likely to appeal to the electorate. No matter. The Left was supporting him, because he had delivered Right support for one of their candidates previously. Prominent Left women accepted and voted according to their faction's prescription. They supported a weak Right man instead of a strong Left woman. After disputation, the man was selected. My own vote, amongst others, was ruled out on a technicality, despite my unbroken and recorded continuous membership of the party since 1971.

Labor did not win the seat. It recorded a particularly low vote. The branch, which had made some mistakes, was humiliated and censured by party headquarters for having the temerity to proceed with a rank-and-file election in the face of a done deal.

This story shows why, until the stranglehold of the factions is broken, the affirmative-action rule for women will not produce the calibre of female parliamentarian, or the woman-friendly and electorally attractive policies intended by the original supporters of the rule. It shows why the current controversy over whether the rule should be changed to require female candidates in 50 per cent of winnable seats has little purchase, and seems to many a diversion from the more urgent need for principled policies clearly stated.

Has Labor changed its male dominant culture? Not much. I don't expect, however, that a female delegate speaking at the National Conference in October will repeat the experience of a woman at a conference in the seventies, trying against numerous interjections to support a child-care policy. "Shut up love and sit down", she was loudly advised by one comrade "or you won't get a root."

In his comments on policy renovation, Button gives perhaps too much weight to Mark Latham's well-publicised policy fragments. The Blair Third Way mantra, which Button disposes of so neatly, is the source of much of Latham's magpie nest of ideas. I am more in tune with the decision of the Chancellor of the Exchequer, Gordon Brown, to put UK Labour back on track by increasing taxes to fund the re-building of the National Health Service. Button identifies the heart of this matter with crystal clarity: "Equality is not just about incomes. It is about fairer distribution of all those services fundamental to human security and development."

Until Simon Crean and his front bench can articulate that principle as clearly, and apply it with practical commitment to education and health in Australia, dozens of rule changes and hundreds of extra seats at the National Conference will not produce a more electable party.

The widely acknowledged fact that standards in our universities are slipping, that students are struggling with huge numbers, decrepit facilities and over-worked and distracted teachers while their fees debts grow heavier each year, was not addressed in any detail by Labor policy before the last election. And still, all Labor offers is criticism, accurate though it may be, of the government's approach. Reassurance for students, staff and researchers has not yet been forth-coming from the party with a great and acknowledged track record in delivering more and better higher education. How long must we wait for federal Labor to grasp the nettle of our increasingly divided schools system? It is simply unac-ceptable to try to educate most of the nation's children in under-resourced schools, especially while the minority at the top end of the private sector suck in more and more public dollars, an injustice that Labor, when given the oppor-tunity in the last parliament, felt unable to resist.

What prevents Crean and his team doing in policy terms what Button and many of us know needs to be done? The answer is now, as it has been since the rot set in over a decade ago: the factions. The factions, so colourfully described in *Beyond Belief*, have for some years controlled everything else in the party. Their hegemony goes well beyond state organisations and administrative committees; it extends to the federal caucus and parliamentary leadership. It has reduced Labor to that pathetic state we used to love to ascribe to the conservatives: a policy-free zone.

Factions are inimical to good policy. Indeed, since their primary purpose is the survival of their faction's power rather than the securing of a reforming gov-ernment, they work against any policy at all. They do not like policy, because any policy that would advance equality of opportunity or fairer distribution of the nation's resources will upset someone. Every focus group (that now ubiquitous tool so beloved of faction operatives) will throw up hostility to any policy worth having.

The Left factions might agree that these comments apply to the Right but claim for themselves more interest in policy and principle. The record shows, however, too many examples of Left and Right colluding out of self-interest against good policy, or to block the selection of the best candidate.

Button is right. Kim Beazley did not fail because of the distressing *Tampa* episode. All the "what might have been" defences, still pointlessly emanating from some Beazley front benchers and party officers nearly a year later, just com-pound the original error. Why did Beazley, a fine human being with a compassionate nature, go along with the Coalition's cruel and ineffective response to the awful events around the *Tampa*? Why does Simon Crean, who has spoken to Australia so directly against child sex abuse, continue in this error? Why does Julia Gillard, who many hoped would early demonstrate leadership potential, often sound more like an apologist for the Coalition than an advocate for an alternative approach based on empathy and strategic judgement?

The answer is that the historic policy strength of Labor, that preparedness to state a principle and then lead the electorate to its acceptance, as both Whitlam and Hawke did in winning office, has been gravely eroded by the impact of the factions. As Button observes, ruling factions produce candidates whose preoccupation is numbers, not ideas. After years of this approach prevailing, the inevitable result is a parliamentary party very light on policy capacity. Just as inevitable, because Beazley never challenged faction power, was the low-risk but disastrous election strategy. The factions didn't want their power threatened by anything that couldn't pass the focus-group test. The factions are still running the show.

What should happen? What do I think is a feasible way out of this quagmire, back to the "light on the hill"? I do not want Labor to spend more years, angrily railing but incoherent and aimless, like Vladimir and Estragon waiting for Godot. Along with other true believers, I want action. Implementation of the Hawke–Wran recommendations could make the party and its processes more democratic, and improve morale. But who would these newly empowered delegates and extra committee members actually be? The danger is, just more of the same mercenaries, as Button calls them, who led us into the bog. Disillusioned members (much less new believers) will not rush to participate in the enlarged and more open structures unless encouraged by inspirational (not aspirational) principles and policies for a better and fairer Australia.

If structural and policy changes happen, and capable and principled people, women and men, can see that selection rules are transparent and fair and that the party knows where it is going, there will be no shortage of good people coming forward. Young people and (I hope) indigenous candidates will volunteer. There will certainly be no need for the crackbrained and discredited idea of drafting "high profile" outsiders.

Now that the nuts and bolts have been addressed by Hawke and Wran, the party's and the media's priority and focus must switch to Jenny Macklin's all-important policy review. It is this, rather than the rules report that presents Labor with its make-or-break opportunity. The Macklin Review is generating plenty of advice. Here is some more.

Typical of party members and Labor voters, I want something better than slight qualifications to mandatory detention and the Pacific Solution. The entire community is waiting to hear how the next Labor government will refurbish the education infrastructure and make access to excellent health care a reality again for all citizens. We're over deregulation. We're over small government. The downside of globalisation must be met by tougher regulation of companies and financial institutions to protect consumers and investors. Because of compulsory superannuation, the latter category covers almost the entire community.

Labor should set out how it will renovate the role of government. Recent experience following Labor-led deregulation and privatisations has shown that while the market does some, but not all, things better than government, it always needs to be scrutinised and regulated on behalf of citizens. The current massive corporate failures, resulting from greed and fraud, create fertile ground for a new definition by Labor of a functional, twenty-first century relationship between the public and private sectors.

The new policy making should use the best advice from all quarters, especially the membership. Avoiding the straightjacket of the focus group it should produce ambitious but realistic reforms. It would be good to hear Simon Crean talking more about Reconciliation and the Republic. These objectives won't get a tick from everyone, but they are essential to a Labor vision, to winning the hearts as well as the minds. Like bringing the factions to heel, they require leadership.

Susan Ryan

Hugh Stretton

In 1984 John Button prompted the Hawke government to commit the Commonwealth's big public utilities to an inventive program of self-improvement designed to lift their performance, justify their independence and defend them from privatisation. He and I were among those knifed in the back six months later when his colleagues dumped the project without any warning to the people engaged in it at home and abroad.

Button is entitled to high respect for his efforts to keep some at least of the social-democratic promises that won the Labor Party its record majority of seats in 1983. Now he tells us what sort of people, with what sort of purposes, broke those promises and degraded the party to the point where

> voters want a real choice and Labor no longer offers them one. The ALP is seen as a pale alternative to the Coalition. It is incapable of embracing and speaking for the divergent progressive groups in the community. It has been unable to respond effectively to new aspirations. It no longer represents contemporary Australia. It may not even represent its members any more: its national body has become an offshore island adrift from the rest of the party, inaccessible to its rank and file, a barren and rocky outcrop untouched by new ideas. (p. 4)

That's what they have become. For what they did to our economy, hear another minister from the Keating government. When Duncan Kerr entered parliament in 1987,

> it was possible to imagine that Australia would resist the seductive claims of globalisation. Australia had high levels of public ownership, including a national bank. Its telecommunications system was

state-owned. It had high (albeit reducing) tariffs to protect local manufacturing. The government had put sectoral industry plans in place for the car and steel industries. Australia had the best system of public health-care in the world. State education was free and there were no fees for entry to university. There were no private universities. The government had the power to regulate the money supply and maintained a fixed exchange rate for the dollar. Most revenue was raised through steeply progressive income taxes.

Just thirteen years later Australia has been transformed utterly. Many changes were wrought by the Hawke and Keating Labor governments ... The conservative Howard government that came to power in 1996 contributed regressive social reform to the mix.

Australia now has low levels of public ownership. Successive governments have sold the national bank and the national airline, opened the telecommunications market to competition and partly privatised the national telecommunications carrier. Tariffs have been reduced to negligible levels. Industry plans have not been renewed. Private health insurance has been subsidised and the public system allowed to run down. The Federal Government now provides more funds to support private education than it provides to assist state schools. Fees or charges have been introduced for the universities. Private universities have been established. Governments have foregone the power to regulate the money supply. The Australian dollar is now a floating currency and the exchange rate is left for the market to determine. Income-tax rates have been repeatedly reduced and a new regressive system of indirect taxation, the goods and services tax (GST), has been introduced.

He concludes that Australia

is now comprehensively enmeshed in the global economy ... The roles of parliaments and governments have fundamentally altered. Many key decisions, which just two decades ago were located at the level of local, state or national governments, are now made by "the market" or by international institutions such as the World Trade Organisation.

This new level of decision-making involves a loss of democratic power. The people who elect me expect me to speak for them and

to represent their interests in government. But, as much real power has shifted to the market and to the institutions of international government, there are large areas where it is increasingly clear that national legislators can be little more than mere spectators.
— *Elect the Ambassador*, Pluto Press 2001, pp. vii–viii

Kerr insists that the Labor governments nevertheless "preserved – to a degree unprecedented in comparable countries, with the possible exception of Canada – the key elements of the welfare state". It would be fairer to say that they prolonged rather than preserved those elements. They financed their welfare measures partly by cutting other useful activities and partly by selling profitable public institutions and services and using the capital proceeds for current spending. They did not establish or continue enough taxation to finance "the key elements of the welfare state" when that windfall was all spent. Nor did they continue former levels of public investment. Among other cuts, Hawke halved the annual capital provision for public housing eighteen months after he had personally promised to double it. (The Keating and Howard governments have cut most of the rest of it, and the states have begun to sell the existing stock.)

What caused the great transformation? Kerr says plainly that national governments freely chose to do it.

Why did an Australian Labor government freely choose to do such a thing? Kerr simply says that "the Hawke and Keating governments went along with the prevailing economic orthodoxy of their times." Respect for prevailing economic orthodoxies is not what drove the creators of the Labor Party or its progressive leaders since. When Prime Minister Hughes changed sides in 1916, plenty of the party did not, and survived to return to office in 1929 with a Labor program. So too when Prime Minister Lyons changed sides in 1931, and when the Split disabled the Labor Opposition through the 1950s. Hawke's and Keating's unique achievement has been to take the whole parliamentary party across to "the prevailing economic orthodoxy", leaving no remainder to re-build – and adapt to our changing times – the social-democratic party that half or more of our people plainly want to have.

(Of course that is disputable. But a solid majority voted for the John Langmore/Ralph Willis program in 1983. And when independent polls have since asked, "would you pay" a specified tax increase if it gave us no waiting time at public hospitals, better state schools, free universities, maternity leave and child care, or other specified value for money, the YES vote has never been as low as 60 per cent.)

Button's essay is on the party. For the policies it lacks but ought to have, he merely sketches some directions: better education, health services, foreign relations, environmental care, enjoyable cities. We should restore the strength of government and its public services, and the independence of judges, the ABC, the universities and "diverse and critical media." "Everyone yearns for a sense of community, to live in a society for which the things that unite people are genuinely greater than the things that divide them ... But the policies are yet to come and they need a lot of thought." (p. 69)

Button wants the thinking to engage the party's members, and the electors of national, state and local government, in serious democratic spirit. He well knows how such social-democratic aspirations have come to be dismissed as old men's nostalgic fantasies. These days "reform" and "progress" are battle cries for further deregulation, privatisation and regressive tax.

But two can play at stealing opponents' slogans. Now that the right are the radical reformers, perhaps the left can succeed as conservative patriots. My purpose in writing this letter is to ask John what he thinks of that project. As follows.

Three lines of reflection in the rich countries come together in the idea of a mature economy. Surprisingly, Australia might be one its pioneers:

- For the first time in human history we produce enough to need no more. But –
- to remove the need for more we must distribute income less unequally, both between rich and poor, and between the years of life in which we earn and the increasing years in which we don't. And –
- we need to replace our dangerously improvident economy with a sustainable one. Moreover –
- pride in some unique elements of our national history might equip Australians, better than most others, to design and carry out such a transformation.

The first of those senile fantasies suggests that we already produce more than enough, and shouldn't *want* to produce any more because it wouldn't make us any happier. All the rich countries now produce enough, if it were appropriately distributed, to give all their members the education they need to get work on fair terms for fair hours in a fully employed economy, with good health and hospital care, and equal justice and civil and political rights. And we produce enough to give *all* our households what three-quarters of them can already afford: a wide choice of household capital to equip them to do whatever they would like to do for themselves, and sociably with kin and friends and neighbours.

We also produce enough to allow desirable inequalities without leaving anyone in poverty. Some people like to compete their way up. Others are easily contented. Some jobs deserve higher pay because they're unpleasant, or specially productive, or demand long education or rare skills. Some self-employed people are best-selling authors, artists, entertainers, inventors. The serious question is not whether we need some inequalities. (We clearly do.) It is what their scale should be.

There have lately been American, Australian and some other studies of relations between income and happiness. In rich countries people in poverty don't average as happy as the rest of the population. But among the rest, income differences don't seem to have much effect on average happiness or wellbeing. That doesn't mean that nobody wants more income than they're getting. What the research finds is that earning $30,000 a year and battling to get to $40,000 seems to have much the same effect on your happiness as succeeding or failing to climb from three to four hundred thousand, or from three to four million.

For believers in our neo-liberal policies, the last twenty or thirty years have seen two embarrassing changes. Average happiness has *declined* with economic growth. And the winners from our inequalities seem to have suffered as much as the rest of us. Declining happiness may also reflect rising numbers of divorces, lone parents, insecure incomes and other upsetting features of our changing times. But twenty years of freer business, economic growth and rising income seem to have left "middle Australia" *and* rich Australians less happy than they were.

Second, we have to learn more than our parents did before beginning to earn, and we live longer in retirement. Fifty earning years had to finance many of them through fifteen years at school and five or so in retirement. Now three times as many of each generation are getting tertiary education, and the average age at death is twenty years above the average age of (often unwilling) retirement. So where fifty years' earnings had to finance about 75 years of life, forty must now finance about 80. Our improving health could reduce the need a bit by allowing longer working lives and later retirement. But without full employment more than half of us are leaving the workforce, many unwillingly, younger than our forebears did. So what should we do – individually and nationally, privately or publicly – to transfer twice the proportion of income that they did from our earning to our non-earning years?

HECS helps a little. (But its repayment threshold should not have been lowered). Compulsory superannuation was meant to help. Commissioned by the

Whitlam government, Keith Hancock designed an outstandingly original, workable, humane and economically benign proposal for compulsory public superannuation. But Whitlam fell before the report reached him. Succeeding governments of both parties have ignored it and developed compulsory private superannuation instead. Dangerously incompetent design and slovenly government allow its managers to take a third or more of many of its members' capital, over and above anything they may lose to market fluctuations. Researcher John Legge concludes that "the privatisers of superannuation have presided over the creation of a league of parasites on a scale not seen since the close of the eighteenth century." Economic growth won't resolve this problem. It demands radical reform of our methods of transferring income over time.

The third imperative is the obvious environmental one. There have been many green initiatives, and creditable improvements, through the last fifty years. The concerns that prompt people to make sacrifices for future generations have much in common with those that inspire social-democratic policies. Far from dividing and weakening the democratic left, might the green movement be its salvation?

It might. But a generation ago, in a paper called "Economics of the coming space-ship Earth", Kenneth Boulding foresaw a different history. The first response to environmental danger would be some green reform. But as it merely slowed and did not stop the loss of resources, a realist second generation would switch to competing greedily for whatever was left.

Reagan, Thatcher and the bipartisan deregulators and privatisers of the Australian economy may have been driven more by bad economic theory and old-style greed than by environmental anxieties. But the effects were much the same, as they dismantled the very capacities of government that effective green reform would depend on.

Boulding expected the green impulse to prosper, then be replaced by its opposite. But both impulses have really been at work, contending against each other, from the beginning. Social-democratic parties still get more votes from those opposed to the neo-liberal shift to the right than do the Green parties. But plenty of people with both purposes vote for the delinquent Labor Party simply because they don't think the minor parties have any hope of governing. A left/green alliance looks promising for both if they can combine effective environmental reforms with a decently progressive distribution of their costs.

It's hard to imagine the Labor Party that John Button describes doing anything with a progressive distribution of its costs. Unlike some of its critics, I don't think it lacks compassionate people with egalitarian values. But they – or their leaders, who tend to be elected by each other rather than by the members – are too scared of "the markets". Business bullies and bad economists convince them that capital, talent and employment will emigrate at the first sign of good government or progressive taxation.

Green and Labor leaders need to think and act as successful progressive parties have always done. Think ahead boldly and, where necessary, inventively. Attack or ignore rich opponents on the right instead of appeasing them. In that spirit, in an economy productive enough to afford all its members the material conditions for happy life, what might a green social-democratic program be like?

It must attempt a lot of things at once, many of them new in purpose or method or both. Besides full employment there are tasks in health, education, trade and industry, financial management, parenting and child care, and in determining how to distribute the cuts in income and consumption that effective green reform is sure to require.

For those inventive purposes, history and the saner social sciences are as important as the natural sciences. How else will we know many rich countries have combined full employment, zero inflation, steeply progressive taxation, reduced and rationed consumption, and long hours of hard work by rich and poor alike, when worse things threatened if they didn't? Or that those wartime achievements may well be possible in peacetime if – this time for environmental reasons – worse must be expected without them? Or that persuasion and experience can change national societies' prevailing values and directions, for good or ill, surprisingly quickly? Or that billions of humans have lived civilised and reasonably happy lives with a lot less household capital and consumption than the rich countries' people average now? And so on through the record of human capacities and incapacities, including social and political as well as scientific and technological capacities. It may even be useful to remember how many defenders of human decency have chosen to die defending it rather than appease or surrender to its enemies. If environmental misuse is going to kill us all, better die fighting it than hurrying it on.

Why indulge such improbable dreams in Australia, the world's second-worst polluter, America's ally in defying the Kyoto agreement?

History again. Our immigrant founders brought the roughest of Britain's working class and the liberal and radical ideas of its best writers and reformers, but – historic blessing! – scarcely any of its upper class. Some of the best of Britain without the worst of it. The radical achievements of the Australian colonies – manhood suffrage, religious equality, women's admission to university degrees, women's rights to vote, women's and Jews' rights to sit in parliament – had all been recommended by British writers and activists but blocked by conservative British governments. Two other achievements, one in the nineteenth century and one in the twentieth, were native inventions. As a sparse population spread over extensive and fairly unhelpful land, one after another necessary service was mooted or started by private enterprise, defeated by the environment, and taken over or replaced by the colonial governments. Then, as native-born Australians came to outnumber immigrants in government and its public services, we became our own inventors. Wage-fixing by independent tribunals. A basic wage indexed to local costs of living. Tariffs to protect wages and the balance of payments as well as to attract and protect employers.

Keith Hancock (a cousin-once-removed of the Keith Hancock mentioned earlier) was a Gippsland boy, son of a clergyman. When he was nine he won a Royal Humane Society medal for saving another boy's life. A scholarship got him to Oxford, then his first job gave him a year in Italy researching a passage of its history for his first book. When he came home aged twenty-six as professor of history in Adelaide, a British publisher asked him to write a book about his native country. In *Australia* (1930) he described attitudes to government, and uses of it, that his British and European experience told him were uniquely Australian. What does the average Australian expect of his state government, for example?

> It is this closer, more intimate Government which protects him from the wicked, educates him, watches over his health, develops roads and railways and water supplies so that he may find permanent employment as a farmer or temporary employment as a navvy, regulates his local trade conditions, inspects his factory – performs, in short, all those functions which seem to affect most nearly his economic and social well-being ... The criterion of needs has been adopted throughout the whole continent. In South Australia, for example, the State Industrial Court is forbidden by statute to award less than a living wage "whatever the consequences may be". Obviously, ethics have once again got entangled with economics. The Australian conception of "fair and reasonable" is ethical, like the medieval idea of the just price. To those who object that such a standard may conflict with economic possibilities, the courts reply that Australia is "not quite so bankrupt in resources of material or of mind or of will" as to be unable to provide for workers "the bare necessities of life in a supposedly civilised community" ...

The Australians have always disliked scientific economics and (still more) scientific economists ... What the economists call law they call anarchy. The law which they understand is the positive law of the State – the democratic State which seeks social justice by the path of individual rights. The mechanism of international prices, which signals the world's need from one country to another and invites the nations to produce more of this commodity and less of that, belongs to an entirely different order. It knows no rights, but only necessities. The Australians have never felt disposed to submit to these necessities. They have insisted that their Governments must struggle to soften them or elude them or master them. In this way they have created an interesting system of political economy ... which embodies the dominating ideas and purposes of the Australian people.

When necessary they had defied the British parliament, the Colonial Office and the monarch. When Hancock's book appeared, they were forcing King George V, much against his will, to surrender his last Australian power and appoint the first Australian, and Jew, to be Governor-General.

If those absent governors oppressed them, weren't they afraid of their own? It was all very well to empower government in a utilitarian way to do dozens of useful things for them. But they seem to have neither respected nor feared their representatives much. "Oppress us? *Those* twits?"

Now the US government and the IMF and the WTO are the bullies. They'll make the attempt to invent a mature economy as difficult as they can. But why don't we lead the world instead of trailing it, or at least die in the attempt?

There would of course be constitutional conflicts. How could we undo the misuses of the treaty power? Nationalise private superannuation? Control the money supply instead of trying to ration it by price? Regulate foreign owner-ship of Australian resources and the uses of foreign exchange? Get effective green clauses into the Companies Act? Or (a personal favorite) extend Industrial Commission awards to all earned incomes, setting minima to those under $100,000 a year and maxima to those above it?

All too hard? How about Duncan Kerr for Chief Justice and John Button for Governor-General ...

Hugh Stretton

John Button

I received a number of letters following the publication of *Beyond Belief*. Most of them were from disaffected members of the Labor Party or former members. Some were depressing stories from people of goodwill who'd tried to join the party and found themselves thwarted by technicalities and "phantom" branches, a product of the imagination of some party bureaucrat. A few letters came from young members with idealistic aspirations frustrated by the heavy hand of factionalism.

Not surprisingly, the essay received some criticism. A contributor to the opinion pages of the Melbourne *Age* took me to task on the issue of the current road to parliamentary selection, arguing that experience in a trade union office was an ideal background for a politician. I am prepared to concede that this might be correct if trade unions affiliated with the ALP were representative of more than a miniscule section of the contemporary workforce. But they are not. It is one aspect of the federal parliamentary membership's retreat from representation of a wide cross-section of the community.

An economist wrote saying that I'd been unkind to economists. He said most of them were good chaps and I'm sure he's right. My criticism was of those economists "who seem to believe that the market can provide universal solutions".

Stuart Macintyre wrote a review in the *Australian Book Review* strangely titled "Missing the Oxygen of Office". Too right, but the ALP needs more than the heady elixir of power. It needs to influence events and provide an alternative vision of Australian society. As he points out, the party "lacks animation". One of the purposes of *Beyond Belief* was to identify the obstructions to achieving a more lively and animated political environment in the party and, as a corollary, in the community.

Macintyre, who sometimes casts himself in the role of an academic pox doctor dispensing potions to the political left, is wrong in respect of one particular historical fact. He writes that as chairman of the 1978 Committee of Inquiry I suggested that "Labor's traditional links with the trade unions had become an obstacle to the social democratic orientation it needed to adopt." This is perhaps an error of convenience, part of the task of positioning himself for his subsequent views, many of which I happen to agree with. "Some have noticed", he writes, "that the diagnosis and remedy bear a striking resemblance to the views he expressed back then." The views I expressed "back then" were that the ALP should have a representative National Conference with delegates directly elected from branches and unions, that the ALP should strengthen its relationship with unions and back the affiliation of unions covering a new and growing section of the workforce. Nothing happened, except for the affiliation of the right-wing Shop Distributive and Allied Employees' Association in the early 1980s. This is a sad fact.

I remember all this pretty vividly, having moved the proposal for national affiliation of unions at the 1979 conference with manifest lack of success. Perhaps, following the Hawke–Wran Report, someone will move it again at the forthcoming conference in October. Its fate will then depend on factional agreement. It could conceivably be passed without debate.

Sadly, because I wouldn't mind being proved wrong, there has been no substantial disagreement with the analysis in *Beyond Belief* of the contemporary Labor Party, of what went wrong in the years of small target strategy and the distancing of the parliamentary leadership from the rank and file.

Barry Jones describes his response as "a supplement" rather than "a rebuttal": and indeed it is. He makes an important point with the rhetorical question, "How important are structural issues?" The answer may well be, as was pointed out in *Beyond Belief*, that they are not particularly important to the average voter. They are, however, important to the party membership. (Interestingly, Jones identifies an active membership of only ten thousand.) In the twenty-first century the ALP desperately needs a structure which facilitates rather than obstructs the free flow of ideas. Members need to feel that they can make a worthwhile contribution. As Susan Ryan points out, "transparency and fairness are essential."

The present federal structure nurtures factionalism, the excesses of which have troubled most commentators, including the Hawke–Wran Review. The question, of course, is what to do about it.

Barry Jones also comments on the phenomenon of Labor hegemony in State and Territory Parliaments. This is interesting but not as important as some people might like to think. Canberra politics determines the direction and character of Australia as a nation. As one commentator pointed out, the Liberals are not conducting a national enquiry as to why they don't succeed in state politics.

Susan Ryan's contribution is an elegant and lucid description of the political culture of the ALP. We are in substantial agreement on most issues. Her reflections on the role of women in the party should be compulsory reading for ALP members of parliament and apparatchiks, simply because it provides a classic illustration of hopes denied. When the 1978 National Committee of Enquiry recommended positive discrimination in favour of women it did so in the belief that more women parliamentarians would lead to a significant improvement in Labor's social policy agenda and the party's understanding of community problems and aspirations. Though women now constitute one-third of the Parliamentary Labor Party, "the discriminatory male thinking and culture of Labor" means that the presence of more women in parliament has had little effect. Women have been press-ganged into the factional system. Already the debate has been twisted into an argument about gender percentages rather than quality of representation and intellectual independence from the dominant culture.

I am very pleased that Hugh Stretton contributed some comments. He has devoted much of his life to the pursuit of good public policy, the identification of real inequalities and social democratic values. His views are always thoughtful and challenging.

He poses one question: "Now that the right are the radical reformers, perhaps the left can succeed as conservative patriots." What do I think? Perhaps, as Stretton points out, this idea is a whimsy of the ageing. I like to think that this is not so; that the values by which Australians used to identify themselves – of an easygoing democracy, egalitarian attitudes and assertive independence – are still capable of being resurrected. It is why in the chapter "Signposts" I emphasised the ongoing importance of an independently minded public service, commitment to public policy solutions which tackle social inequity and waning institutional integrity, the priority of environmental care and an independent foreign policy. It is also why I bemoan Labor's retreat from the bush where it seems to me that many of these traditional values are alive and well and the idea of community care and involvement remains strong.

Hugh Stretton calls this "pride in some unique element of our national history". He suggests this might equip us to approach the challenges of over-production, unequal distribution and a "dangerously improvident economy". These are huge issues for public policy which will not be readily embraced by the political parties. The record is not good. After all, Hugh Stretton put some of them on the agenda in *Capitalism, Socialism and the Environment* published in the late seventies. They remain valid as directions which what Stretton calls "mature economies" will be forced to come back to.

David Day, the perceptive biographer of Curtin and Chifley, has contributed a thoughtful essay on the more recent history of the ALP which relates back to what I believe to be enduring values established by Chifley. Kenneth Davidson suggests that the major recommendation in *Beyond Belief* is "a disaffiliation of the unions". As I pointed out in the *Quarterly Essay*, the limelight always falls on this question when the question of restructuring the Labor Party arises. The main argument of *Beyond Belief* is that the present union affiliation makes the Labor Party less representative rather than more representative of the broader spectrum of Australian society. Factionalism has abused the system of union affiliation in a manner which I suspect is more damaging to the unions than to the ALP. As an idea, I floated the example of the Swedish model, which seems to have been beneficial both to unions and the political party. It is the sort of issue which should be discussed in a progressive Labor movement.

Davidson is sceptical about the possibility of reforms when they are in the hands of vested interests which benefit from the present system and his scepticism is illustrated by some good examples. I too am sceptical, but as I said in the foreword to the essay, it was written "to point out what might be possible, as distinct from immediately achievable". To this I would add, with the wisdom of hindsight, that the issues set out in *Beyond Belief* should always be up for debate.

John Button

John Button was Leader of the Hawke and Keating Labor governments in the Senate from 1983 until his retirement from politics in 1993. Over the same period he was Minister for Industry, Technology and Commerce. He is the author of *Flying the Kite*, *On the Loose* and *As It Happened*.

Kenneth Davidson is a columnist for the *Age* newspaper and the co-editor of D!SSENT magazine.

David Day is a senior research fellow in the history program at La Trobe University and the author of biographies of John Curtin and Ben Chifley.

Barry Jones was National President of the Australian Labor Party from 1992 to 2000. He is the author of several books including *Sleepers Wake! Technology and the Future of Work* and the *Dictionary of World Biography*.

John Martinkus is an Australian investigative reporter on the Asia region. In 1999 he was nominated for a Walkley Award for his coverage of the violence in East Timor. His book *A Dirty Little War*, an eyewitness account of East Timor's struggle for independence, was shortlisted for the NSW Premier's Literary Awards in 2002.

Susan Ryan became in 1983 the first woman to hold a cabinet post in a federal Labor Government and from 1984 to 1987 served as the federal Minister for Education and Minister Assisting the Prime Minister on the Status of Women. Her political autobiography, *Catching the Waves*, was published in 1999.

Hugh Stretton is a research fellow in economics at Adelaide University. His most recent book is *Economics: A New Introduction* (UNSW Press, 1999).

www.ingramcontent.com/pod-product-compliance
Lightning Source LLC
Chambersburg PA
CBHW081400270326
41930CBC0015B/3370